CW01337610

Giggleswick School Chapel

NOEL PROUDLOCK

ISBN 0 9517185 1 7

All rights reserved.
No part of this book
may be reproduced or transmitted
in any form or by any means,
electronic or mechanical including
photocopying, recording, or by any
information storage or retrieval
system, without the permission of
the publisher in writing.

© Noel Proudlock 1997

Published by J. N. D. Proudlock
181 West Park Drive (West)
Leeds LS8 2BE
Typeset by Ink Rays
Printed in England by Pindar plc Preston

A CIP catalogue record for this book is
available from the British Library

Frontispiece
The Architect's drawing of the Chapel from the North East
courtesy Giggleswick School

Contents

Foreword

by Anthony P Millard BSc (Econ) FRSA
Headmaster, Giggleswick School

The first glimpse of Giggleswick I had was of the Chapel Dome as I drove down from Buckhaw Brow. Since becoming Headmaster many people have asked where I regard the centre of the School. The answer is simple. It is the Chapel that Old Giggleswickians first wish to see when they revisit us with their families and friends. When much else is forgotten it is the communal experience of music, reflection and worship in this wonderful building which floods back to the memory. Now that it is nearly a hundred years old the Chapel is in need of thorough restoration and much of the work has been made possible by the great generosity of a number of Old Giggleswickians to the Appeal. But the Chapel is not a museum. It is a place of regular living worship in which today's generation of pupils seek the same inspiration and awakenings as did their predecessors. Walter Morrison's gift and T.G. Jackson's design endure and will continue to be the focus of the School's spiritual life in the next millennium. Noel Proudlock's careful research and recollections will be of lasting value to understanding the history of Giggleswick and I have great pleasure in commending his book to all its readers.

New Chapel
Giggleswick School
Yorkshire

T. G. Jackson R.A
Architect

5

Preface

Giggleswick School Chapel has not braved the Pennine weather on top of its rocky knoll since construction began in 1897 without feeling the effects. So in early 1997 very expensive major renewals of, and repairs to, the outside fabric have been completed whilst refixing the mosaic inside the dome is underway and further major renovations inside the Chapel and elsewhere on the site will be started as sufficient funds to complete them are in place. The response of the Old Giggleswickians to the Chapel Centenary Appeal has shown clearly how much they value, and the great affection in which they hold, this most memorable of the School's buildings. I am no exception having been bewitched by it from the first moment I stepped inside, an enchantment remaining undiminished to this day.

I felt some recognition of the events of 1897 ought to be given and provided an article for the March 1997 issue of "Dalesman" to acknowledge the centenary of Walter Morrison's announcement that he wished to give a Chapel to the School also to be its Diamond Jubilee Memorial. In undertaking some of the research for that article in the School library it quickly became clear that there was a fund of information available to explain those interesting events much more fully, describe a notable building in some detail and relate its history during its first century in a well illustrated book.

The School authorities were happy to make everything in their library, especially the Brayshaw collection, and elsewhere, available to me and I must acknowledge the extensive help given to me by the Librarian, Mrs Barbara Gent also the Bursar and Clerk to the Governors, Mr Denis Smith and his staff in particular for loan of a copy of the presentation to the European Union. Mr Don Hutton, Publicity Manager, for loan of the more recent photographs shown "courtesy of Giggleswick School" and Mr Ian Shevill for loan of the older photographs shown, "courtesy Giggleswick School (Brocklebank collection)". I must also thank the Headmaster, Mr Anthony Millard, for his support and giving his permission for all this and for consenting to write a Foreword. A photograph of the Royal Observatory party at the Chapel for the Solar Eclipse of 1927 has been supplied by them and permission given for its reproduction.

A major source of information on the materials used in construction of the Chapel and the designers and manufacturers of the many beautiful features inside was "Giggleswick School, Notes of the History of the School and an account of the New Chapel" published without imprint, printed in Oxford by Horace Hart, printer to the University, dated 1901 and presented to guests at the Dedication Service. The copy in the Brayshaw Collection in the School Library is endorsed "W. Bateman, 7th October 1901" and inside

> "Giggleswick Chapel
> Foundation Stone laid 7th October 1897
> by the Duke of Devonshire K. G.
> Chapel opened 4th October 1901
> by Dr Warre, Headmaster of Eton
> Dedicated by the Bishop of Ripon"

The writer of any history is more than fortunate when so detailed and authoritative a contemporary account is available to him.

This book, then, is my tribute to a very special building published to mark the centenary of its Foundation Stone being laid.

Leeds, April 1997   *Noel Proudlock*

Plate 1 By October 1897 the walls were above ground level and preparations for the Foundation Stone Ceremony were made.

courtesy Giggleswick School (Brocklebank Collection)

Plate 2 The crowd at the Foundation Stone Ceremony.

courtesy Giggleswick School (Brocklebank Collection)

CHAPTER 1

Origins

Giggleswick Village, lying to the west of the River in the lower part of Ribblesdale in Yorkshire is an ancient settlement and has been the home of the School of the same name since 1512. It was founded by James Carr of Stackhouse, Priest of the Rood Chantry in Giggleswick church as a 'Gramer Scole' and when King Henry VIII died and that means of foundation ceased it relied for a time on local people for support. John Nowell, Vicar of Giggleswick and Chaplain to King Edward VI was instrumental in obtaining a new charter for the School from the King, dated 26th May 1553, which endowed it with certain lands, tenements and rents securing its position. It was thus able to continue as a small establishment, very much in the clerical tradition, with Latin and Greek the dominant subjects and the Master required to address the older scholars "only in Latin". This was the situation for more than 350 years until a major change in the foundation structure became possible at the time of the Charity Commissioners scheme of 1864 which included the creation of a much larger Board of Governors. These changes allowed the School to expand and the number of pupils grew rapidly.

Sunday worship was an essential part of School life and the small numbers involved before 1870 could easily be assimilated into the normal congregation of St Alkelda's Church in Giggleswick village. But the growing numbers put a strain on this arrangement and in 1875 the Vicar of Giggleswick agreed that the School could hold separate services in the church. This expedient overcame the immediate problem but there were those who realised that it was not a wholly satisfactory long term solution.

One of those joining the enlarged Board of Governors in 1864, indeed he had attended meetings before being formally accepted as a member, was Walter Morrison MP of Malham Tarn House. He was a man of wide international business interest and of great wealth which he had inherited as a young man and which he believed should be used in the furtherance of education and for other philanthropic purposes. It is known he made gifts to Oxford University, Bodley's Library, the University of Leeds and King Edward's Hospital as well as giving systematically to many other charities. He completed his education at Oxford where he was an excellent oarsman and rowed stroke to the Balliol eight at the Head of the River. On that occasion there was a minor accident when a boat in which Thomas G. Jackson was an oarsman was in collision with Morrison's boat. This bump, minor on the normal scale of events, had great significance for Giggleswick in the years to come.

After leaving Oxford Morrison made the Grand Tour visiting Palestine and Egypt, gaining a lasting fascination for those countries, becoming one of the earliest members of the Palestine Exploration Society and founding a Chair of Egyptology at Oxford. In the business world he played a significant part in developing trade in South America as a major shareholder in the Central Argentine Railway including thirty years as its Chairman.

Thomas G. Jackson, after going up to Oxford, won a scholarship to a different college, Wadham, and after completing his course thought of becoming a painter but instead took the perhaps more practical step of joining Sir Gilbert Scott's Architectural Practice in 1858. He began to practise himself in 1862 and in 1864 was elected a Fellow of Wadham College. His work was largely in educational establishments, ten principal public schools including Eton (Laboratories and the Club House on Queen's Eyot), Harrow, Rugby (The Speech Room) and Westminster whilst at Oxford he designed the City High School and the High School for Girls. He also undertook work for several Oxford colleges, his reputation there founded especially on the New Examination Schools but he was also responsible for the New Brasenose Buildings and the New Radcliffe Library. At Cambridge he designed the Law Library, the Sidgwick Memorial Museum and Laboratories whilst his work can also be seen in London at Drapers Hall and the Inner Temple. He was also a builder of churches, mainly in the South of England, and undertook considerable restoration work. A particularly interesting commission he received, as a result of a great interest he had in the Dalmatian coast, about which he wrote a book, was to restore the campanile at the Cathedral of Zara, a work completed in 1892. Amongst his church restoration work was the renewal of faulty foundations at Winchester Cathedral and the associated building of a new row of buttresses. It was particularly in recognition of this

Plate 3 Construction in progress – the walls well above ground level.
courtesy Giggleswick School (Brocklebank Collection)

Plate 4 The building takes shape – the ring of the dome complete.
courtesy Giggleswick School (Brocklebank Collection)

Plate 5 Inside the dome during construction – the first ladders and scaffolding.
courtesy Giggleswick School (Brocklebank Collection)

Plate 6 A view of construction work in progress.
courtesy Giggleswick School (Brocklebank Collection)

work that he was later made a Baronet. He was an associate of the Royal Academy from 1892, a full member from 1896 and also an Associate of the Royal Academy of Belgium. In 1910 he received the Gold Medal of the Royal Institute of British Architects. He died in 1924 aged 89.

These seemingly disparate strands came together in a most memorable way through the Diamond Jubilee of Queen Victoria's accession to the Throne, the major national event of 1897. The kind of memorial to be provided to honour the Queen's remarkably long and notable reign was a topic of discussion by all kinds of institutions in cities, towns and villages throughout the British Empire and at Giggleswick the School authorities were no exception. In fact they were having great difficulty reaching a decision what to do but on 1st March their debate was ended very abruptly by a letter from Walter Morrison MP at Westminster to the Headmaster, the Rev. G. Style. This first event in the history of Giggleswick School Chapel is reproduced in full:

"The House of Commons
1st March 1897

Dear Style
    I have an idea in my head of offering to build the School a Chapel with a dome as an architectural experiment employing Jackson, the famous Oxford Architect. One would call it the Diamond Jubilee Memorial. Site the Knoll in the Cricket Field. We have very few domes in England and it might give a hint to others.
    But I should like to have any suggestions of yours. A domed building on the site should look well. It would need much thinking about as we do not understand domes. The Round Church at Cambridge gives some hints.

    Yours truly
    W. Morrison."

Although it is recorded this was the first the School knew of Morrison's intention, Jack Brassington, OG. recalled how his father, who was involved in the construction work, accompanied Morrison to look for a site and when they saw the rock out-crop beside the cricket field Morrison said "We'll have it here, Brassington."

The speed at which events then moved did not accord with Morrison's expectation of how difficult it would be. The Governors, a major problem solved, enthusiastically accepted the offer. A formal presentation and acceptance took place on 26th March and the next day the Headmaster announced to the School that a Chapel was to be built for them as a gift of Walter Morrison. On 2nd April 1897 Morrison and Jackson visited Giggleswick to look at the site "on the knoll by the cricket field". In fact Jackson had worked swiftly after Morrison first secretly approached him and had made sketches enabling him to define the exact site on which the Chapel would stand during this visit and express his complete satisfaction with the situation his building would occupy.

There was now every need to make haste to have the Foundation stone laid during the Jubilee year. Site preparation occupied April and May but in the middle of June Richard Evans arrived to occupy the position of Clerk of Works working directly under Jackson without the employment of a contractor, except that labour in carpentry and joinery was contracted for by Brassington Bros. and Corney of Settle. Work began in earnest and rapid progress was made with the foundations and the lower part of the walls which showed above ground level by the end of September.

Jackson's drawing of the Chapel's Northeast elevation had been shown at the Royal Academy exhibition whilst the Headmaster had sent it to Balmoral where, on 4th October, the Queen and Princess Beatrice admired the design of this impressive memorial to her reign. The time had arrived for ceremony.

So on 7th October 1897 the Foundation Stone was laid with suitable dignity. Events began with a luncheon at which Morrison entertained those involved in the ceremony, the School Governors and other guests. During the speeches after the lunch Morrison explained his motives in deciding to make the School this notable gift, saying he had offered the Chapel to the School because he desired to increase the prosperity of the School and a Chapel was part of the proper plant of every large School. All over the country fountains and clock towers and hospitals and halls were being built to commemorate the (Jubilee) day. All those were good. So he had asked himself if he could not do something to add interest to this beautiful country where he had lived so many years and which he loved so well. He had offered the Governors a School Chapel as a memorial of the Diamond Jubilee of the Queen. At the same time he was able to gratify a whim of old standing, that of building a dome if he could find an excuse for doing so. He had travelled in many lands where domes were frequent features in the landscape and the dome seemed to him the most beautiful as it was certainly the most scientific mode of roofing a space which had been devised by man. Very few domes had been built in England and he had to choose an

Plate 7 The workforce posed in front of the West Wall and Rose Window.
courtesy Giggleswick School (Brocklebank Collection)

15

Plate 8 Another view of the West Wall during construction.
courtesy Giggleswick School (Brocklebank Collection)

Plate 9 The building taking shape photographed from the South-East.
courtesy Giggleswick School (Brocklebank Collection)

architect. So he went to the famous Oxford architect Mr Jackson. Of all English architects he thought he was the man who was most likely to make an experiment a success. He asked Mr Jackson if he would design for him a dome and Mr Jackson replied by asking if he remembered his rowing, forty two years ago, at Oxford, in an eight oared boat which bumped the head boat of the river, of which he (Morrison) was the unfortunate stroke. That bump still rankled in his breast but Mr Jackson had undertaken to make him some amends for the humiliation which he then inflicted on him by building him a Chapel which should be worthy of his fame, worthy of the magnificent site, worthy of the traditions of the School. They meant the workmanship to be good, that it should rival the fine work of English workmen of the last century.

Jackson also addressed the gathering and said that, by the intention of its munificent founder, Giggleswick School Chapel was to be no ordinary Chapel. When Mr Morrison had called on him he had asked him "are you disposed to consider an architectural experiment – people are generally shy of experiments and seek safety in precedent?" He naturally welcomed the opportunity. Mr Morrison desired that a dome should be the motive and Jackson said he had worked from that to the rest of the design. At the same time he felt it to be important not to break with the traditions of their native English styles. And it became an interesting problem to try and combine the oriental feature of a dome with Western Gothic. His old Master, Sir Gilbert Scott, he remembered in one of his Academy lectures, had expressed his longing to try his hand at a Gothic dome. He never, however, had the opportunity for which, Jackson further said, he had to thank Mr Morrison for trying the experiment. The result was now before them on paper and he hoped in another year they might have it before them in stone sufficiently advanced for it to explain itself. And they would see, he trusted, an English building which, in spite of its swelling dome, would not be out of keeping with its surroundings in the Yorkshire dale which, from its lofty rock, it would command far and wide.

After lunch the principals and guests climbed up to the construction site for a service and the laying of the Foundation stone. The service was conducted by the Bishop of Ripon before a congregation composed of the Governors and their friends, many present and past members of the School and many visitors. The Foundation stone was then laid by the Duke of Devonshire who spoke afterwards saying how pleased he had been to take part in the ceremony, how much he appreciated Mr Morrison's gift and offering his good wishes for the continued prosperity of the School. Thanks on behalf of the boys for his presence and his laying of the

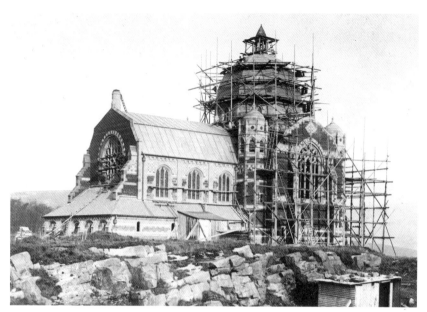

Plate 10 A further view of the growing building from the South West.
courtesy Giggleswick School (Brocklebank Collection)

Plate 11 The finished building viewed from the North East.
courtesy Giggleswick School (Brocklebank Collection)

18

stone were given by the Head Boy, J. T. Macnab, and on behalf of the Governors by their Chairman , Hector Christie. The stone is located quite low in the outside wall at the North East of the nave, as is traditional, inscribed to commemorate both its laying and Queen Victoria's Diamond Jubilee as follows:

TO THE GLORY OF GOD
AND IN COMMEMORATION OF
THE SIXTIETH YEAR OF THE REIGN OF
VICTORIA QUEEN AND EMPRESS
OF THE BLOOD ROYAL OF
ENGLAND'S DARLING
ALFRED THE KING
THIS STONE WAS LAID BY
SPENCER COMPTON CAVENDISH
DUKE OF DEVONSHIRE, K. G.,
ON 7th OCTOBER 1897.

With these celebrations successfully concluded the Architect, Clerk of Works and craftsmen could have the site to themselves to complete their work. Four years were needed but at the end of that time a wonderful addition to the landscape had been created, a building about which there has been much conjecture amongst those seeing it from afar and in which there is much pride amongst those lucky enough to see it at close quarters or, better still, attend services in its remarkable interior.

Plate 12 Walter Morrison, whose idea and gift the Chapel was.
courtesy Giggleswick School (Brocklebank Collection)

Plate 13 Thomas G Jackson, the Architect who made Morrison's idea into a realisable plan.

courtesy Giggleswick School (Brocklebank Collection)

21

Plate 14 Richard Evans, the Clerk of Works, whose skill made the plan reality.
courtesy Giggleswick School (Brocklebank Collection)

CHAPTER 2

The Building

Morrison's determination to have a dome and Jackson's stylish incorporation of one into his overall design resulted in a building which cannot be overlooked. Those who do not know what it is often think, no doubt because of the dome, that it is an observatory, others imagine it must be some other kind of religious building but all notice it as Jackson predicted in his 1897 speech. The dome is covered on the outside in copper sheeting which exposure to the weather, through oxidisation, turned green. Many have conjectured how it must have looked when new, but renewal, as described in Chapter 6, was completed before the manuscript for this book had to be finalised and in early January 1997 a copper coloured dome again dominated the scene. It will turn green again and the conjecture now is how long it will take.

The knoll which Morrison selected as the site for the Chapel is of millstone grit and to the west of the chosen position a quarry was established, its site now hardly visible, to provide the stone for the walls. This does not show, however, as it is faced both outside and inside with other stone. All the visible surfaces are of carefully selected materials from a wide variety of places, those covering the inside from world-wide sources. The outside facings to the walls are yellow Idle sandstone up to the plinth and above it red Lazonby sandstone decorated by bands and chequers of sandstone and black limestone from Horton-in-Ribblesdale. The wrought masonry outside, including the window traceries, is of Lees-moor sandstone, a material of great hardness and durability. The copper covered octagonal dome dominates the roof but there are also four sections of main roof originally covered, and in 1997 again re-covered, in cast lead whilst green Elterwater slates provide cover for the side aisles and west end antechapel.

Plate 15 The Rose window in the West Wall.

courtesy Giggleswick School

Plate 16 Detail of one of the sections in the Rose window.

courtesy Giggleswick School

24

Plate 17 The East window.

courtesy Giggleswick School

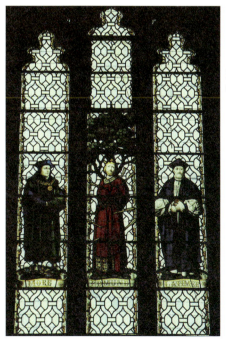

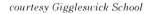

Plate 18 An example of the clerestory windows – More. Edmund. Latimer.
courtesy Giggleswick School

The materials combine to produce, from a sufficiently close viewpoint a wonderfully subtly coloured building.

Beneath its dome it looks compact and chunky, well set to withstand the weather in its exposed position, with pronounced east, north and south facades linked by turrets at each corner and together with the nave forming the shape of a Latin Cross. The lie of the land makes it very convenient to have a vestry below the east facade with an independent entry. An internal staircase leads from this into the body of the Chapel.

But the beautiful external appearance is no more than an apéritif to the splendour of the interior. It was Morrison's clearly stated desire that the Chapel should be built and fully furnished as a single design concept within one construction period so that no opportunity would exist for any unsympathetic additions at a later date and this wish has been respected during the Chapel's first hundred years more rather than less so in recent times. Morrison and Jackson had knowledge of and access to a range of choice materials, eminent designers and artists and quality workmanship with which to produce a superb, dignified yet outstandingly beautiful interior. The walls mirror the outside colours but with stone from different quarries, being Ancaster Oolite banded with red Egremont sandstone. The floor is of marble, principally black and white, the white from Serravezza and the black from Mazy in Belgium. Beneath the dome is a panel of coloured marbles, the mosaic borders made from "verd'antico" from Casambala in Thessaly and porphyry coloured "Rosso" from Scutari in Laconia. The central disc is of red Pavonazzetto breccia from the Isle of Scyros in the Cyclades whilst the four smaller discs are one each of Irish green from the Lousouter Quarry, Recess, Galway and yellow breccia from Stazzema, Tuscany and two from the Cipollino quarries at Stura in Euboea. This marble is named after its green laminations which resembled the markings of an onion (Latin cipolla). There is a small bronze cross in the central red disc which marks the exact centre of the dome above.

The windows feature some beautiful painted glass made by Burlison and Grylls to designs by the Architect and Sir James Linton RWI. The east window shows the life of Christ. The centre is a figure of Christ in Glory, to the right the Sermon on the Mount and to the left the Ascension. Below these, from left to right, are the Annunciation, the Salutation, the Angels appearing to the shepherds, the Visit of the Magi, the Presentation in the Temple, the Flight into Egypt and Christ among the Doctors. Below the three principal illustrations are the following inscriptions rendered in Greek: "King of Kings, Lord of Lords", "Consider the lilies of the field, how they grow; they toil not neither do they spin"; "Peace I leave with you, my peace I give unto you" and under the seven smaller ones "Strive for the truth unto death and the Lord God shall fight for thee. Be not hasty in thy tongue and in thy deeds slack and remiss".

The great window in the south transept has illustrations drawn by Sir James Linton of people important in the development of the School. That in the middle light is Edward VI copied from an illumination in the charter given by him to the School, below is James Carr of Stackhouse who founded the School in 1512 and the other lights show Walter Morrison holding a model of the Chapel, Archdeacon Shute, Archdeacon Paley and the Reverend George Style, Headmaster in 1897.

The west Rose window illustrates the creation and was made from a sketch by the Architect.

Sir James Linton also designed most of the figures in the six clerestory windows above the nave. Each window contains three figures to a theme, on the north side Martyrs, Sir Thomas More, King Edmund, Bishop Latimer; Divines, Bunyan, Wycliffe, Wesley; Teachers, Alcuin, Wykeham, Arnold; on the south side warriors, Sir Philip Sydney, King Alfred, General Gordon; Missionaries, Henry Martyn, Columba, Livingstone; Poets, Milton, Caedmon, Tennyson. Mr T. J. Grylls of the firm which made the glass designed the figures of Sir Thomas More, Sir Philip Sydney and General Gordon.

Two niches over the internal West Door are occupied by bronze figures by George Frampton A.R.A., one of King Edward VI and the other of Queen Victoria. He was regarded as the foremost sculptor of the time and upon the death of Queen Victoria was commissioned to provide statues of her for Leeds, Southport, Newcastle, St Helens, Calcutta and Winnipeg. Perhaps his most famous work is the statue of Peter Pan in Kensington Gardens.

There is extensive decoration of the wall and ceiling areas in sgraffito work. This was done to the Architect's designs, by two of his pupils from Oxford, William H. Nicholls of Hertford College and Douglas Stewart of Oriel. This form of decoration involves the use of two layers of plaster, a base one of whatever colours are required for the pattern and a thin top coat of whatever overall colour is required. The top coat can only be applied to the extent it can be worked on the day as the pattern is pricked or pounced through a full size pattern or cartoon and the still soft plaster scraped away to expose the coloured coat underneath. In this case pink and green are used as the undercolour with white as the overall colour to create vine and scroll patterns and also inscriptions in Latin. Each of the four vaults which support the ring on which the dome sits are

Plate 19 The mosaic of St. Matthew on the NW pedentive.

courtesy Giggleswick School

Plate 20 The mosaic of St Mark on the NE pedentive.

courtesy Giggleswick School

28

Plate 21 The mosaic of St Luke on the SE pedentive.

courtesy Giggleswick School

Plate 22 The mosaic of St John on the SW pedentive.

courtesy Giggleswick School

especially fully worked with a sacred monogram in the centre of the arch and labels carrying inscriptions regularly interspersed in the pattern. The nave ceiling is similarly decorated but to a reduced extent only providing borders to the several sections of the roof. Inscriptions are also placed around the nave below the clerestory windows and round the ring of the dome. There is also sgraffito work on the antechapel walls.

All the interior woodwork is cedar, extensively carved, all but a small proportion imported personally by Morrison, no doubt as a result of his connections with and knowledge of the country, from Tucuman province in Argentina. It is of especially fine quality, colour and scent and has a peculiarly silky sheen of great beauty. Both the north and south transepts have galleries made from this wood, that on the north side accommodating the organ and that on the south seating, both reached by semi-circular stairways in the east end turrets. Below these galleries seats backing the outside walls are provided for visitors and in front of these are the choir stalls including the customary provision for officiating clergy and with scrollwork enclosing the supports for the galleries. The central part of the nave is occupied by pews for the scholars but the rear row, backing the antechapel wall, is raised and comprises four stalls on each side of the wide central aisle and double west doors to the antechapel. They have carved and pierced standards to their canopies containing figures of the four evangelists writing their gospels and attended by their emblems whilst in the canopies above are pendants with figures of six prophets, Moses, Elias, Esaias, Jeremias, Ezekiel and Daniel. Access to the scholars pews from the outside aisles is through a colonnade with the capitals of the pillars carved to represent foliage of plants common in the locality.

Most of this can be seen whilst entering by the West Door and walking down the central aisle but very soon the eye is drawn upwards to see superb mosaics. These cover the pedentives between the vaults and the inside of the dome and were made by Powells of Whitefriars to a colour scheme devised by the Architect and using cartoons by George Murray, a student and medallist of the Royal Academy. Powell's Foreman and craftsmen had previously carried out the mosaic decoration in St Paul's Cathedral to the designs of Sir W. B. Richmond.

The eye first sees the four pedentives where the full curved triangular space of each is used to portray, on bordered gold backgrounds, the Evangelists, seated, with their respective emblems. Above that is a vertical ring of stonework with pillars and windows before the dome itself starts to curve inwards. This is fully covered by mosaic work in three ringed sections. The lowest also has a gold background and shows sixteen angels rather more than six feet high, playing musical instruments, with their wings outstretched and overlapping to form an interlacing pattern of fine and varied colour. The middle section is of sunset tinted clouds with flights of birds, whilst for the final one the background changes to a deep blue with a circle of cherubs round the eye of the lantern. The whole effect is quite stunning.

Sir Walter Parratt, Master of the King's Music and organist of St George's Chapel, Windsor, was engaged by the Architect as his consultant to draw up the specification for the organ and to superintend its construction which was undertaken by Henry Willis and Son of London. This was probably the last instrument built under the supervision of Henry Willis since he died before it was completed. Those pipes which can be seen from the interior of the Chapel are partly screened by carved cedarwood at their tops whilst their bases stand on carved cantilevers projecting from the panelling forming the front of the gallery, thus being most effectively incorporated into the overall decorative style of the building. The full specification is given in Appendix 3.

Lighting was by gas. Ten very elegant brass chandeliers, each with seven mantle arms and made to a design by the Architect were suspended from the cross rafters and the ring below the dome. So that adequate light was available for reading hymn, psalter and prayer books by the occupants of the pews the chandeliers were fixed perhaps twelve feet above the floor. The effect was very pleasing and, I can say from personal experience, gave a beautiful warm glow to the interior. A heating system using hot air was installed, its generating equipment being placed in a vault below the antechapel.

The Architect designed an impressive lectern made in bronze by Hart, Peard and Company of Drury Lane, London comprising a shapely stand surmounted by an eagle with outstretched wings, the back of which provide the reading desk. It occupies the customary position in the cross aisle between the nave and the choir to the right of the centre aisle when looking from the West Door.

All this took four years work to complete but during September 1901 construction work came to an end, the Architect's drawings became reality as he had promised and the building did indeed "explain itself". The aims of both the Commissioner and the Architect have been described earlier and there can be no doubt that they were fulfilled in an outstanding way. As well as wishing the Chapel to be constructed as a complete entity Morrison also wished to see the whole site planned and developed and therefore commissioned Jackson to design two further buildings. The first

Plate 23 The outside ante – chapel wall showing the green Elterwater slates, Red Lazonby sandstone and yellow Idle sandstone 14 th September 1996.

author

Plate 24 Detail of the mosaic on the inside of the dome.

courtesy Giggleswick School

Plate 25 Detail of the Angels forming the bottom section of the mosaic in the dome.

courtesy Giggleswick School

was a gatehouse situated where the Chapel's access road joins the Giggleswick village – High Rigg road at the top of what is, not surprisingly, now known as Chapel Hill. This comprises two storey living accommodation to the east side of and above the archway and storage accommodation to the west. It was completed in 1906 and occupied by Mr and Mrs Parker, the first of a small number of long-serving occupants who have also been custodians of the Chapel. A tuck shop was incorporated into the building from the outset. Boys had been visiting village shops to make this type of purchase and it was said at the time that significant benefit would derive from ending that practice. The Gatehouse continues to be occupied by a member of the School staff, although the tuck shop has now gone.

Beyond the Gatehouse the access road passes the cricket field and then becomes a broad footpath climbing the Chapel knoll by a series of steps interspersed with short rising sections. The cricket field lies to the south and west of the Gatehouse and the second building was a stone built pavilion in traditional style having a clock tower and situated at the west end of the field. It stands at a somewhat higher level with a flight of steps leading down to pitch level. This building also remains in use without any external alteration.

It now only remained to celebrate the completion of the building work and formally bring the Chapel into use. This took place on 4th October 1901 during an impressive ceremony. Dr Edmund Warre, Headmaster of Eton, was invited to be Guest of Honour and it is, I imagine, no coincidence that he too was an oarsman in the Balliol boat at Oxford when that collision occurred. It really was a bump with far reaching consequences for Giggleswick. The proceedings started at 12.30 when the Governors walked in procession to the West Door of the Chapel where the Bishop of Ripon and the clergy were assembled. Mr Morrison handed Dr Warre a silver key with which he ceremonially opened the door. He then gave an address and at its close asked the Bishop to dedicate the Chapel to the service of God with the words "Right Reverend Father in God on behalf of the Governors of this ancient and religious foundation, and particularly at the request of Walter Morrison, founder of this Chapel, I ask you to dedicate this place to the service and worship of Almighty God." This was duly done during the course of a full and impressive service and afterwards the guests assembled in Big School and then went down for luncheon in the covered playground which had been most handsomely decorated for the occasion. The Chairman of the Governors, Hector Christie, took the chair and after the boys had joined the gathering toasts and speeches were made. The Bishop in the course of his address said he thanked Mr Morrison for having entered a practical protest against that sort of utilitanarianism which entirely forgets that the most useful things in the world are often the most beautiful and the most beautiful in their turn are often the most useful. The gift of that Chapel was not merely a beautiful gift which delighted the eye of the beholder but was an educational gift to inspire future generations. Thomas Jackson's remarks in response to the toast to him are particularly worth repeating – he said that no more inspiring scheme could have been offered to an architect than the one set before him. He had a beautiful site surrounded by a lovely landscape and he had no anxiety about the cost. Everything had been of the best and nothing had been forgotten. In "The Times" obituary in 1924 it was said that Jackson's most remarkable work was Giggleswick School Chapel.

Sir Walter Parratt was also present for the occasion and at 4.00pm, as a finale to the days celebrations, gave a recital in the Chapel on the organ he had designed. The programme is given at Appendix 4. These events concluded, the Chapel could begin to establish its special place in the life of the School.

Plate 26 A view on14th January 1997 as the scaffolding was being removed and the Chapel looked as nearly as possible as it did when first completed.

author

Plate 27 Interior showing part of the organ and sgraffito work.

courtesy Giggleswick School

Plate 28 The Chapel from the South. 6th July 1996.

author

CHAPTER 3

The First 50 Years

The School possesses a wonderful collection of books, including bound volumes of the School Chronicle and other local publications, press cuttings, photographs and other memorabilia made by Thomas Brayshaw, an OG, local solicitor and Clerk to the Governors for many years. The collection covers the period from the building of the Chapel when he was at School up to the thirties and was presented to the School in 1964 being housed in a special section of the library. In the case of the Chapel several of the architects own drawings of the building inside and out are included. Research into this treasure house of information has revealed little about the Chapel after its dedication. This is not, perhaps, surprising as its function in School life is inherently routine however superbly the building is equipped to fulfil its role. However, the School Chronicle does report several services to mark special events during the first twenty years.

As might be imagined 1902 saw the first anniversaries acknowledged. On 4th October a special service was held in the Chapel at noon to mark the first anniversary of the Dedication Service, a sermon being preached by the Headmaster. Three days later on 7th October the fifth anniversary of the laying of the Foundation stone was celebrated by an evening of special events. A supper was held in the Dining Room during which the Headmaster made a toast to Mr Morrison who was greeted with an enthusiastic response. This was followed by a concert in Big School.

When, at the start of my researches, I first saw the Architect's drawing of the Chapel's interior I noticed immediately that the lectern was not in its present position and the pulpit was not shown. This latter puzzled me since it is such an essential part of a church's furniture and the one in the Chapel in no way looks like a later addition. The mystery was partly solved by an item in the Chronicle reporting that a service was held in the Chapel on 9th November 1902 to "inaugurate the new pulpit". The guest preacher that day was the Rt. Rev. J. J. Pulleine DD. Bishop of Richmond and the writer of the Chronicle report commented "It is satisfactory to find that the School can now hear the preacher much better than previously". What I have not yet discovered is where sermons were preached from before November 1902 and why preachers might not have been heard. Presumably it was from the choir stalls, probably the one opposite that from which services are traditionally conducted in churches or from the lectern in its original position in the centre of the choir but in my personal recollection no difficulty was experienced in hearing anything said from any of those positions. Of course the Architect's assertion in his response to the toast to him on Dedication Service day that nothing had been forgotten had now been shown to be not quite correct!

This first and only major addition to the Chapel needs description. It is located in front of the main pillar to the Northeast of the nave and is reached by a short flight of steps facing from east to west. It is of carved cedar, to match the rest of the building. The plan is hexagonal with the upper panels decorated in an unusual way, effectively pierced work, whilst round the upper edge of the panelling is a pendant cornice of original design. Above is an octagonal canopy, noticeably greater in spread than the lower structure to meet the acoustic requirements of the building, with each corner being surmounted by a pinnacle. These pinnacles are joined by elaborate pierced galleries whilst the lower part of the pulpit is linked to the canopy by a carved panel fixed to the stonework and inscribed on its upper part "Predica verbum insta opportune importune". In my days at School I was always rather glad not to have been in my near namesake house, Nowell, whose pews were immediately below the pulpit and over whose younger occupants the preacher must have towered quite overwhelmingly!

The next event meriting a report in the Chronicle was the preaching in the Chapel of a farewell sermon by the Headmaster. The Rev. George Style had announced he would retire at the end of the Easter term 1904 bringing to conclusion a most successful tenure of the position. He became Headmaster in 1869 when there were just two boarding pupils and had organised and overseen an unprecedented growth in the School including construction of the buildings which form the core of the present establishment. It was particularly fitting that the Chapel should have been completed during his time as Headmaster ensuring that the School lacked no appropriate facility when he handed it over to a successor. In his

38

sermon he called to mind the time 30 years earlier when the School first joined together as a separate body for public worship in the old (Giggleswick Parish) church. The report of the rest of the sermon was the recollection of the writer in the Chronicle and the Editor remarked that, with characteristic modesty, the Headmaster had destroyed the notes of this notable farewell sermon "and so frustrated the general desire to possess it in permanent form". This event perhaps marks the end of the first phase in the Chapel's life.

Other events interposed but here is perhaps the appropriate place to record that George Style died on 16th January 1922, aged 80, and proposals were mooted to have a memorial to him in the Chapel. On 1st November 1922 eight Old Giggleswickians – The Rev. G. J. T. Harker MA., of Aldenham School, Elstree, The Rev. J. R. Wynne Edwards MA., Leeds Grammar School, J. J. Brigg MA. Kildwick Hall, Keighley, A. H. Blundell, Charles Johnson MA. Arthur Hacking OBE., Norman McQueen DSO. and J. B. Ogden MA – circularised all other OGs and the School to say that no positive proposal had been submitted and that they were setting up a fund to obtain the necessary money. Sufficient was quickly donated, a tablet was designed, made, put in place and unveiled by the Rt. Hon. E. L. F. Wood MP during a special service in the Chapel on 7th July 1923. It is located to the south side of the altar and, apart from the 1939-45 war memorial is the last to have been placed inside the Chapel. A full list of memorial plaques is given as Appendix 5.

Meanwhile a major milestone in the School's history was reached on 12th November 1907, being the 400th Anniversary of the day James Carr signed the lease for the plot of land by St Alkelds's Parish church in Giggleswick village on which the first School was built and the first recorded date in connection with the School. Several events were arranged for so special a day including a Thanksgiving service in the Chapel with the sermon delivered by a special guest preacher, the Rev. Samuel Bickersteth DD., Vicar of Leeds. New Fives Courts were opened that day and also a new metal workshop given by J. G. Robinson, a Governor of the School at that time. Finally a recital was given on the Big School organ by Plunkett Greene.

It was also at this time that the dormitories, previously known as A, B, C and D were given their now familiar names celebrating those important in the School's earlier history, Carr, Nowell, Shute and Paley. Interestingly the two additional names chosen for new houses subsequently are those particularly associated with the Chapel, Style (in 1938) and Morrison (in 1966).

Plate 29 The Chapel overlooks games – in this case cricket at Eshtons.

courtesy Giggleswick School

Plate 30 The Chapel overlooks games on the cricket field.

courtesy Giggleswick School

A sad event in the Chapel on Sunday 31st May 1908 was a memorial service for Gifford Bromley Mannock who had died on 26th May 1908. He had been a much respected master at the School for 34 years and it is, of course, relatively unusual for a master to die "in service". The Headmaster preached a sermon in his memory and a tablet was placed in the Chapel acknowledging his long service to the School so sadly terminated.

After this event the Chronicle had no more reports of special services although I do not suggest this means there were none rather that the Chapel's role in School life, even in connection with special events, had become so well established that they were no longer thought worthy of description. A notable exception was 21st July 1912 when the 400th Anniversary of the opening of the first School on 21st July 1512 was celebrated.

The Chapel had a period of national fame from a surprising source in 1927 and brought the name of Giggleswick right to the fore, even into that bastion of Englishness, "Punch" (see Appendix 6). On 29th June that year it was predicted that a total eclipse of the sun would be visible in England along a line from Southport to Hartlepool. Giggleswick lay exactly on the line and the School authorities offered the Astronomer Royal, Sir Frank Dyson, use of the field to the south of the Chapel to set up his instruments, which he gratefully accepted. The eclipse was expected to last from 0520 to 0715 with total obscurity at 0624 for a period of 23-24 seconds. Huts to house the instruments, including a giant telescope 45 feet long and a spectroscope, were provided by the School and the Officers Training Corps provided guards to protect them. The Royal Observatory party arrived two weeks beforehand and the best Pennine summer weather, continuous cloud and strong wind, severely hampered their work in setting up the instruments which required continuous spells of sunshine. Everything was satisfactorily installed, however, and, despite some misgivings reported in the press during the run up to the event, the wild Pennine wind round the Chapel did not blow down the temporary huts or damage the telescope. The bad weather continued to the last minute so that it remained doubtful whether the eclipse would be visible, but luck was with the Giggleswick party, if no-one else, and a break in the cloud occurred at the vital moment.

The results of the observations from the Chapel field were communicated in the Notices of the Royal Astronomical Society Vol LXXXVII No 9 in a "Report of the Expedition from the Royal Observatory Greenwich to observe the total solar eclipse of 1927, 29th June (communicated by the Astronomer Royal)." This described the observations planned and commented that in the event there was an adequate break in the clouds so that the programme of observations could be fully accomplished and the Astronomer Royal expressed his thanks (amongst others) to the Governors and Headmaster of Giggleswick School for the use of what the exigencies of weather made the best site in England.

A contemporary press cutting titled "Eclipse Dejection" emphasised the remarkable luck of the Astronomer Royal by describing the experience of a reporter who thought he might enjoy a better view at Buckhaw Brow than the official party at the Chapel. Cloud obscured his vision at the critical moment and he was described as "one of the saddest men in England" when he learned that the view from the Chapel had not been affected by the cloud so short a distance away.

The Astronomer Royal paid tribute to the press for drawing attention to the rare occurrence of total eclipses and the splendour and impressive nature of the spectacle. The LMS and LNE Railway companies had arranged many special trains to various places along the line of totality and many more travelled by car and charabanc. The local police Superintendent estimated the number of visitors in the Settle area to have been 100,000.

Use of the Chapel grounds by the Astronomer Royal in this highly publicised way no doubt gave strength to the idea in the minds of many who did not know what the Chapel was that it was an observatory. The final event in this brief period of fame was receipt at the School of a hand-written letter of appreciation from the Astronomer Royal to the Headmaster:

1927 June 30

The Royal Observatory
Greenwich

Dear Mr Douglas,
    I should like to thank you and the Governors of the School for all the help we have received. The site you lent us was an excellent one anyway and proved to be the best in England. We appreciated very much the advantage of being in a field where the instruments were safe during the fortnight of preparation and the excellent arrangements by which the OTC kept us from any interruption at the time of the eclipse. The observers would like to say how kind and obliging Mr Parker was to them.
    I hope you will come and see us at Greenwich when you are in London.

    Yours sincerely
    F. W. Dyson.

Plate 31 The Astronomer Royal's party in the field to the South of the Chapel. Sir Frank Dyson is standing third from the right.

by permission of the Syndics of Cambridge University Library and of the Director of the Royal Observatories

The Chapel returned to its sober routine existence and the silence of the Chronicle regarding any special events continued. Maybe in those hard times in the thirties there were none.

The Second World War brings this period of the Chapel's story to a close but one requirement of those years, blackout, introduced something which continued as an important part of Chapel tradition when peace returned. Although the building was still lit by gas the number and height of the windows, including those in the lantern above the dome, coupled with the Chapel's dominating position ensuring any light would be seen for miles in every direction, meant that blacking-out was both impracticable and essential. The only option was to hold those services required in winter after daylight by candlelight, a practice continued afterwards for a late evening last night of term service. This was developed by Mr E. H. Partridge, Headmaster during my time at School, into a service calculated to enhance the Chapel's place in the hearts of Giggleswickians in a way which continues and grows after they leave and makes it the focus which it is for their affection for Giggleswick.

Some years later this idea was introduced to Catteral Hall for their annual carol service, held separately from that for the senior School. This also was held by candlelight, with the service memorised by the boys – a tougher task for the young Catteral Hall boys than for an end of term service in Big School – and included a mime giving a "spooky" ambience to the event so appealing to small boys. Both these services have now fallen out of favour but some hope one or both may be re-introduced. I hope so too and chapter 4 may explain why.

Plate 32 The North West aspect of the Chapel on 14th January 1997.

author

Plate 33 The Chapel on a summer's day 22nd May 1949.

author

Plate 34 The Chapel on a winter's day 9th December 1949.

author

CHAPTER 4

Recollections

My personal association with this wonderful building began on Sunday 20th September 1945, the first Sunday I was at Catteral Hall, the Preparatory School, when I was 11. We set off in a crocodile down the drive, past the pretty waterfall, along the road behind the Headmaster's house and up the very steep Chapel Hill. At the top, a bit out of breath, we turned through the Gatehouse arch, crossed between the cricket field and tennis courts, climbed the steps and entered the Chapel. Inside we passed along the south side aisle, climbed the spiral stone staircase in the Southeast turret and filled the long pews in the balcony. All I could see appealed to me and I would very much have liked to take a close look at everything, especially the south window behind me. Who were all those people depicted in it? However as a new boy I felt that gazing around might not be too well received and so I concentrated on the inscriptions in view and the organist in his loft on the opposite side. In fact it was several years before an opportunity arose to look around the building thoroughly since the Sunday ritual walk there and back afforded no scope for individual activity. I could not wait for my mother's first visit so I could share this marvellous place with her and wrote to her that evening "The Chapel is as nice inside as it is outside. How nice that is you will see when you come on 20th-21st October because you'll come to morning chapel with me that Sunday and every other Sunday you come as well. The organ is enormous. Mr Partridge usually takes the service, or has done so far." When the day came she did indeed share my enthusiasm and derived great pleasure from attending many services over the ensuing years. I could not say that I was a devoted churchgoer before the day described above nor have been since I left School but I would never have sought an excuse to miss a service in the Chapel and still relish an opportunity to attend one in it today. The fact is that the appeal of the building and the style of service during my days there has not been matched anywhere else I have been able to go.

After a year I moved up to the main School and started to attend two services each Sunday now, of course, sitting in the main body of the Chapel in the Carr House pews towards the rear of the right hand side. The services were the customary matins and evensong, their conduct shared by the Chaplain and the Headmaster and with a lesson read in rotation by the School seniors sometimes, it has to be admitted, showing their nerves at this very special kind of reading in public. The form of service was straightforward and without any frills with a sermon delivered only in the evening, usually by the Chaplain but from time to time by the Headmaster and very occasionally by a guest. On occasion I found sitting through a fairly lengthy sermon somewhat of a problem, especially in winter when the warmth inside the Chapel contrasted with a cold afternoon spent "out of hostel" and have to admit to having been less than wide awake at times when the sermon ended and, prompted by the noise of others standing up, doing so myself more by habit than intention.

In those days Sunday morning service in particular was a major item in the School week. We made our own way up to Chapel but it usually happened that the great bulk of boys set off at about the same time to arrive comfortably before service time. To be late was unimaginable. School dress for Sunday at that time was dark blue suit, blue shirt, black tie and, when necessary, navy blue raincoat plus, of course, hated School cap. Most masters also attended and for them gown and hood were "de-rigeur". This was also the service most visiting parents attended since it was after it that we were released from School routine to be taken out.

Mention of visiting parents brings to mind how cars were much less powerful in those days and gear changing rather more difficult than today. Chapel Hill is very steep, narrow and hemmed in by a high retaining wall on one side and Hostel Rocks on the other creating a blind corner. The path, with steps, now made inside the wall up to the Gatehouse was not there in the late 40s and we walked up the road presenting an additional hazard to car driving parents (there was the occasional avant-garde mother even then). We had to stand to the side of the road as they came up and used to notice and discuss how they coped with the driving demands of the hill and woe betide the boy whose parent made a botch of it! After the service the Headmaster left first, followed by the masters and boys and parents and it was a colourful scene with the masters

Plate 35 The interior from the East end with a service in progress – the lesson being read, showing clearly the new chandeliers.

Plate 36 The interior from the West, again with a service in progress and the lesson being read.

courtesy Giggleswick School

viewed from behind so that the colourful part of their hoods showed and mothers dressed for the occasion among the boys as this procession moved down the steps and along the path between the cricket field and tennis courts until it stretched from the Gatehouse arch back to the Chapel.

Each week after Saturday morning assembly in the main hall, "Big School", which was equipped with an organ, the whole School spent a short period studying the hymns and psalms for the Chapel services the next day. The music master of the day wanted everyone to take part in the singing and understood only too well how much care was needed to avoid something little better than a raucous noise from an all boy congregation. This extended to widening the repertoire so that from time to time part of the session was spent learning a new tune, chant or even setting of the Te Deum, Magnificat or Nunc Dimittis. In the latter cases a "unison" version would be sung by the congregation. These practices greatly increased enjoyment of the services.

At this time the Gatehouse was occupied by Mr and Mrs Cresswell. He was the Head Groundsman but also had care of the Chapel, holding the keys and being responsible for opening in time for services. He also had the job of lighting those seventy gas mantles, which he did using a long pole. The School Seniors, or Praeposters – I was never quite sure which was really their correct title – waited in the antechapel to escort visitors to their seats and Mr Cresswell stood with them ready to open and close the nave doors for teaching staff or very special visitors. He would also escort to the visitors seats any latecomers who arrived after the School Seniors had taken their places for the service, sometimes parents arriving, to their sons' acute embarrassment, after the service had started. The Gatehouse still accommodated the Tuck Shop now presided over by Mrs Cresswell selling home made cakes and pastries and a small range of sweets. This was not too onerous a responsibility since it was open only from 4.00pm to 5.00pm on Tuesdays, Thursday and Saturdays and during the winter terms boys playing rugby on the more distant pitches hardly had time to get back to School, have the bath essential to remove the mud and climb up to the Gatehouse before tea!

The start of the Autumn term in September 1947 brought us a shock! The seemingly unchangeable had changed and the Chapel now had electric light. Gas light had become very outdated, the change to electricity having been delayed by the war in many places whilst maintenance was becoming increasingly difficult. The new lighting consisted of fluorescent tubes positioned as inconspicuously as possible consistent with providing adequate illumination.

Plate 37 Looking through the West Door.

courtesy Giggleswick School (Brocklebank collection)

However, this style of lighting was in its infancy and a rather harsh pinkish light resulted, by no means as pleasing as the gas, and it was not really well received. The tubes were positioned in pairs inside the clerestory windows in the nave, and singly along the side aisles and under the galleries to light the visitors seating and rear choir stalls. Lighting was also provided for the gallery and organ loft and further tubes were installed behind the south arch to illuminate the altar. Mr Cresswell no doubt found operating one or two electric switches a much more acceptable task than tending those seventy gas mantles.

Another task, this one undertaken by two boys, which disappeared at the same time was manual pumping of the organ. I never knew, or discussed the task with, those who undertook it so cannot say what they did when the organ was not required, for instance during the sermon, but there were tales, probably apocryphal, how, as a result of nodding off or becoming too engrossed in a book, air was not available when needed and the sound of furious pumping could be heard. I did pump the Big School organ for George Briggs to practise not least because I particularly like organ music and enjoyed hearing him play. With "full organ" in use it needed some effort to keep the marker weight steady indicating to the pumper that adequate pressure was being maintained.

Now when the Chapel organ was needed after prayers or the sermon the switching in of the electric motor, installed at the same time as the lights, was audible as was the sound of its working until the organist began to play. The Chapel was not quite the same any more.

I do not remember that any recognition was made at the time of these modernisations that it was 50 years since building had begun nor in 1951 that it was 50 years since the dedication service, although I had left School by the October anniversary date.

A major event for me in the Chapel was Confirmation. The first confirmation service in the Chapel took place on Friday 12th December 1901, conducted by the Bishop of Ripon when 24 candidates were presented. The next was on 20th June 1904 and thereafter mid summer continued to be the season for this ceremony. In 1950 candidates were sought, as usual, to attend classes held by the School Chaplain culminating in a Confirmation service in the Chapel. There was considerable interest, well into double figures and, being at School, few if any, dropped out. When the classes were completed there was a practice session in the Chapel to ensure everyone was well rehearsed and on Sunday 11th June Dr. Blunt, Bishop of Bradford, came to the Chapel to perform

Plate 38 An interior view during the period when the lighting was by fluorescent tubes and there were no chandeliers.

courtesy Giggleswick School (Brocklebank collection)

Plate 39 Morrison commissioned two other buildings on the site – this is the Cricket Pavilion seen on 14th September 1996.

author

Plate 40 The other building was the Gatehouse, here seen on 6th July 1996.

author

the ceremony. We went up in pairs to kneel before him at the alter for the laying on of hands and the blessing. My companion was Stephen Hanscombe. Those important events in life which include a religious service do not typically take place during schooldays and so I was particularly pleased that this one which does could be in the Chapel.

At the end of each autumn term the traditional twelve lessons and carols service was held in the Chapel – and still is I am pleased to say – and this always enjoyable occasion could be savoured at its best in this beautiful setting. However, the Christmas celebrations were expanded in November 1947 by a performance of "Messiah" in the Chapel and my recollection is that this was an innovation by the then quite new music master Dr. H. L. Smith. So that the whole School could take part and no-one would have to be just a listener certain of the best known sections were sung by everyone in unison and to ensure this was successful several practice sessions were arranged as well as parts of the usual Saturday morning practice period. At that time the Chapel choir trebles were led by John Senior who had a much above average voice which lasted well into his teens and his singing of the soprano arias gave us great pleasure. Paul Ryley was also a soloist and when, nearly fifty years later, in 1995 I met him during tea served on the cricket field on OG/Old Parents day before we attended a short service in the Chapel I reminded him of that event. He responded "It was the most frightening day of my life!" The performance was regarded as a success and on 2nd December 1948 there was a performance of "The Creation" followed on 17th November 1949 by "St Matthew Passion".

For Christmas 1950, however, something more ambitious was planned. "Messiah" was chosen again but guest singers were invited for some of the solo roles as well as a guest organist so that Dr. Smith could conduct both choir and congregation. The Chapel choir was augmented for the performance and a series of special choir practices arranged whilst the usual Saturday morning sessions to preview Sunday Chapel music were expanded to include the "congregation" parts as had been the case in 1947. These preparations culminated on this occasion in a full rehearsal in the Chapel with the guest organist although not the soloists. School routine was rarely changed but on Thursday 23rd November the normal afternoon sports period was allocated for the practice and the Chapel's customary calm and dignity suffered something of a shock. Dr. Melville Cook, at that time Musical Director at Leeds Parish Church, was the guest organist and the event went well enough until the first section when the whole School had to sing

54

was reached. Dr. Cook was playing in a style appropriate to accompany a trained choir and Dr. Smith quickly realised this was entirely inappropriate for some 250 boys enjoying a lusty sing. His problem was how to stop organist and singers. He abandoned all decorum, raised both hands above his head and shouted "whoa!"

The singing quickly stopped , the organ music petered out and a very surprised Dr. Cook popped his head out of the organ loft saying "what's the matter Dr. Smith?" "Full organ please, Dr. Cook" was the reply. "Full organ (heavy emphasis on "full") queried Dr. Cook. "Yes" said Dr. Smith, "they'll never stay with you otherwise." Dr. Cook withdrew with a rather puzzled expression but brought in full organ and all went well. The performance was in the evening on Monday 27th November and was both successful and enjoyable. My special recollection is of Jack Brassington's performing of the tenor arias. I had heard him sing before, to me unforgettably as Nanki-Poo in Gilbert and Sullivan's "Mikado" which we were taken to see from School, as a rare treat, at Settle's Victoria Hall (another Diamond Jubilee building, no doubt) performed by the Settle Amateur Operatic Society. I have been a devotee of those wonderful operas ever since.

At this time I was in my second year in the Sixth form and my regular attendance at Chapel services was moving inexorably to its close. In particular I realised I had only three more last night of term services to attend, although in the event I missed the March 1951 one by leaving before the last day of that term to be Best Man at my Uncle's Easter Wedding. It was a very carefully and cleverly designed service, always exactly the same, even to the organist's voluntaries, and held with illumination from just two candles on the altar. The Headmaster, in my days E. H. Partridge, read the prayers and lesson by torchlight and I knew I was not alone in finding it very special. On one occasion I remember particularly clearly the night was mild, still and clear with a full moon and several of us went up early and stood on the highest point of the Chapel knoll admiring the moonlit view over Settle to Attermire Scar, absolutely clear in those pre-sodium street-light days in the bright moonlight, until it was time to go in for the service. It was, of course, necessary for the whole School to know the whole service by heart and after several years I almost knew the lesson (Ecclesiastes Chapters 11 and 12) by heart as well. At the end of my last service in July 1951 the blessing "Go forth into the world in peace" seemed unbelievably pertinent and wherever I am if I hear the "Londonderry Air" or "Nimrod", the opening and closing voluntaries at the service, I am immediately transported to the Chapel and that emotive service.

During my National Service I was stationed in Berlin and as, by then, those that had been juniors during my last year at School were now the Seniors and would themselves be leaving I had the notion to attend one more "End of Term" service. A fortnight's home leave over Christmas 1953 made it practicable to be at Giggleswick on the night and the fact that the service was held in the dark made it possible for me to enjoy it as I had been accustomed from the Carr House pews and not from the visitors seats which would not have suited my purpose at all. The House Seniors of the day agreed to squeeze up to let me join them. So two and a half years on I savoured my final 'last night of term' service. I was not disappointed.

Plate 41 The view across Settle to Attermire Scar from the Chapel Knoll – 6th July 1996.

author

CHAPTER 5

The Second 50 Years

I little thought as my personal close involvement with the Chapel ended that nearly 50 years later my recollections might form a link between the first and second 50 years of the Chapel's first century. Those second 50 years have seen changes which would have pleased Walter Morrison and Thomas Jackson as well as one or two they would never have imagined possible when they designed it – electricity and girl pupils, not to mention the clay pigeon range just outside the West Door.

The use of the Chapel for memorial services for those who devoted themselves to the School over many years, for Thanksgiving services and for performances of religious choral works was by now thoroughly established in the fabric of School life. A lengthy listing of the latter would no doubt be tedious but, for instance, on 20th November 1952 the Bach cantata "Sleepers Awake" was performed whilst on 2nd December 1954 it was "Messiah" once more, although extracts only on this occasion but with Dr. Melville Cook and Jack Brassington again this time joined by Mrs Haygarth, a local soprano. On 22nd November 1955 Handel's setting of Dryden's "A Song for St Cecilia's Day" was the choice, again with Dr. Melville Cook but Edward York, tenor, and Mary Collice, soprano, as the soloists. After this mention of such events in the Chronicle ceases for a time.

In November 1957 the first important addition to the School buildings for many years, apart from the seriously necessary toilet block of the late 40's, was completed. This comprised extensions to the laboratories and new class rooms and to mark the event on the 30th of that month a service of Thanksgiving was held in the Chapel attended by all those who had taken part in the construction work. Afterwards they were entertained to dinner.

My Headmaster, E. H. Partridge retired in July 1956 after a quarter of a century at the helm. I endorse wholeheartedly a part of the Chronicle editorial about his leaving which read "The Chapel, perhaps, is where we shall remember him most .... but above all at a time when he is most likely to remember us – at the end of term service when we are told to proclaim ourselves one house, one brotherhood".

His predecessor, the Rev. R. N. Douglas died during the spring of 1957 and a memorial service for him was held on 11th May, conducted by Canon W. Byron-Scott who had been School chaplain during his Headmastership. Mr Partridge himself, whose health was known no longer to be of the best when he retired, died in March 1962 and a memorial service for him was held on Saturday 31st March, conducted by the Headmaster and the Chaplain. The Second Master who had been at the School longer than Mr Partridge and had worked closely with him as his Second Master for the last eighteen years of his Headmastership, gave a moving address which was later printed in the form of an obituary. During 1963 the Old Giggleswickians Club provided a reading desk for the Chapel as a memorial to Mr Partridge, most fitting in the light of the remarks in the Chronicle quoted earlier. Thus within five years nearly half a century's Headmastership had had to be recalled and honoured. It was perhaps fitting that 1962 was the 450th Anniversary of the founding of the School.

Giggleswick seems to have had an extraordinary effect upon its Second Masters this century in terms of long service and longevity. There have been only three spanning three quarters of it, H. M. F. Hammond, L. P. Dutton and W. R. Brooks, just so recently retired, whilst the position has now been superseded. Mr Hammond ended his career at the School in 1945 to enjoy fourteen years retirement until his death in May 1959. A Memorial service for him was held in the Chapel on 30th May but Mrs Hammond wished to see his long service to the School acknowledged in some more tangible way. So, firstly, in the early part of 1961 she presented to the School a brass tablet in memory of her husband which was placed on the Second Masters stall at the rear of the Chapel which he had occupied for so many years. There followed some quite lengthy correspondence between Mrs Hammond and the Headmaster about installation in the Chapel of additional seating in the aisles during which the Headmaster said how pleased he would be to see the "deal benches with which we have had put up for so long" replaced. This was also accomplished in 1961 by the provision of fixed seating along the outside walls of the side aisles, made of cederwood to match the original centre pews to which it is adjacent and carrying the inscription "H. M. F. Hammond 1896-1945".

A direct connection between the Chapel and the Civic life of the area was created in 1961 when Mr Cresswell was elected Chairman of Settle Rural District Council and also in that year he and Mrs Cresswell attended a Garden Party at Buckingham Palace. This was towards the end of his 33 year long service to the School and, as occupant of the Gatehouse, the Chapel since he retired in 1962. Occupants of this position have, like Second Masters, been few in number and long serving. In the 56 years 1906-1962 there had been just two.

Settle had a festival week in September 1964 and, as befits a building so dominating the landscape, the east end of the Chapel which, of course, faces the village of Giggleswick and the town of Settle, was floodlit during that week whilst on the 25th of the month W. H. Stalker and F. A. Jackson, of the staff, gave a recital for oboe and organ as part of the week's festivities.

The organ had been maintained by Messrs Willis and Son since they had completed its construction in 1901 but by 1960 over half a century of hard work had made more than routine maintenance necessary. Just as Sir Walter Parratt had drawn up a specification and given advice when the organ was constructed so Dr Francis Jackson, the renowned Musical Director of York Minster, was retained to give advice on the reconditioning and considerable alterations and additions were made, still keeping the basic nature of the instrument Sir Walter Parratt had specified. The work was completed during 1961 and on 15th July Dr. Jackson gave a recital comprising works carefully selected to show the organ's potential which the Chronicle reported had indeed "demonstrated how powerful and diverse an instrument it now is". The programme is given as Appendix 7.

The maintenance contract was transferred to J. W. Walker and Sons in 1973 and by 1975 it had become apparent that after 75 years hard use the perishable parts of the organ, leatherwork and feltings needed cleaning and restoration. This work was carried out by J. W. Walker and Sons during 1976 and great care was taken that the renovations, as far as practicable, restored the organ to its 1901 condition.

Despite its improved condition there was an item in the 1994 Giggleswick School News Sheet that "The Chapel organ met its match". This was a report on a recital given by that extraordinary organist Carlo Curly in his own exuberant style, waving from the organ loft with his handkerchief, calling it the flight deck and the keyboards the flight console. So that the audience could watch him

Plate 42 The Gatehouse seen from the South East 14th September 1996.

author

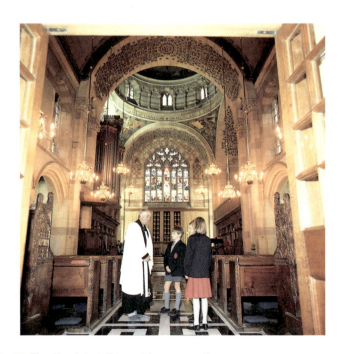

Plate 43 The Chaplain talking with some pupils.

courtesy of Giggleswick School

at the console, Ian Shevill, the current occupant of the Chapel Gatehouse and a very proud and caring custodian of the Chapel set up an arrangement of video cameras and a large screen. I have previously described an event which, at the time, I thought was somewhat of a shock for the Chapel's customary calm and dignity. This, I am sure, was very much more so in a very different way and I wish I had known of it and been able to be there.

The Chapel was built to commemorate the 60th year of Queen Victoria's reign and it was therefore particularly fitting that the 60th Anniversary of its dedication should be specially marked by a Celebration Service on 4th October 1961. The Provost of Bradford preached at this important event in the Chapel's history with the report in the chronicle more detailed than many previous items and suggesting that some similarities between the two services had been arranged. I do not think I can improve on what was written at the time to describe the occasion and it significance:

"Both congregations stood in the Chapel high on its bleak knoll dominating the surrounding countryside. But the Chapel is not only an impressive building but also a house of prayer. There can never have been a boy at the School in the last sixty years who has not regarded the Chapel as his own. This is our Chapel wherever we might be, however far from it, an abiding possession and a lasting joy to us all.

A fine building though the Chapel is, we must not forget that the church is made of living stones. The beautiful building in which we worship every Sunday is the effective sign of our common life"

The 75th Anniversary was also celebrated but in a different fashion and the Headmaster announced the intended service in advance in the 1976 Giggleswick Bulletin in a way which reflected the changing times for religion in schools. He wrote under the heading "Spiritual Values", "Rarely put into words,. but I think implicit, is the desire of parents that the Christian faith should be presented to young people : parents feel that before long many maintained schools will abandon the teaching of Christianity in favour of, at best, comparative religion and, at worst, secular humanism or even Marxist atheism. Thus during the weekend of the Old Boys Autumn Re-union on Sunday 26th September we shall gladly celebrate the 75th Anniversary of the opening of our School Chapel welcoming parents, Old Boys and friends to our morning service at 10.15am at which the new Bishop of Ripon the Right Rev. S. Hetley Price is to preach".

Perhaps the Chapel's place was seen to be a little at risk at this time.

This 1976 Anniversary came just a little too late to make possible what might have been a remarkable return to the Chapel. C. H. Tattersall died at the Hest Bank, Morecambe, aged 87 on 14th October 1975. He had been a Chapel chorister and had been a soloist at the dedication service in 1901 and was most probably the last living link with that event amongst those who took an individual part.

It was a very happy coincidence indeed that the Chapel's 75th Anniversary year was also Architectural Heritage Year. H. R. H. The Duke of Gloucester and Sir John Betjeman, the Poet Laureate, made a series of celebratory visits throughout the country that year one of which was to the School and included the climb up to see the Chapel.

Services from the Chapel have been broadcast on several occasions, the first record I have found being on 25th October 1953 when morning service was used for a North Regional programme. The service was conducted by the Rev. J. E. Anderson and the Headmaster preached a sermon, unusually of course for morning service as it was customary for the sermon to be in the evening.

By the nineties outside television broadcasting has become the accepted way of providing much of what is offered for viewing and in 1991 the School and its Chapel featured in a service televised nationwide. BBC Radio again broadcast services from the Chapel in the Summer of 1994 when recordings were made for no less than three programmes; The BBC World Service, Radio 4 Morning Service and Radio 2 Sunday Service.

Confirmation services in the Chapel had, since the second one in June 1904, been held in Summer but a change was made in 1959 when there was a reversion to the December date of the very first one. The Bishop of Bradford arranged to stay overnight and conduct a Service of Holy Communion the next morning which, I am certain, would give added significance for those attending their first such service.

In 1980 the Headmaster wrote in the Bulletin that the Governors had felt able to agree to an increase in the number of scholarships, although to a maximum rebate of one-third of the fees. These included choral scholarships which, as Giggleswick was one of the few boarding schools to have a pupil age range from 8 to 18, would start in Catteral Hall and extend into the Senior School. He continued "We hope thereby to take some advantage for ourselves .... to build up a choir that will keep alive one of the glories of English musical inheritance − its church music". The Chapel, through its services, could expect to be a major beneficiary of this initiative. No quick dramatic results could derive from it but,

Plate 44 The Duke of Gloucester in the Chapel grounds during the Architectural Heritage year visit. *courtesy Giggleswick School*

Plate 45 The Princess of Wales with school pupils during her visit.
courtesy Giggleswick School

whether there is a connection or not, and I have not researched this issue as it really is peripheral to the Chapel's story, events since 1990 have certainly brought Giggleswick Chapel choir to the notice of a very wide audience. For instance they sang during 1991 in York Minster, Chartres and Notre Dame and in late 1993 gave concerts in Paris, Strasbourg Cathedral, St. Thomas's Strasbourg and the Church of St. Joseph, Colmar. During the period three tapes/ Compact Discs have been commercially produced, "Christmas at Giggleswick", "Magnificat" and "Sing Joyfully" with tracks from the last named being played on Classic Radio FM on several occasions soon after its issue.

1986 and 1987 were vintage years for the Chapel with a range of events requiring the Chapel and its grounds to be used for almost every kind of special occasion, starting with a second taste of national media coverage. In nearly 60 years since the 1927 Eclipse media techniques had advanced unimaginably so that coverage of a Royal event made the 1927 press presence seem very low key! H. R. H. The Princess of Wales visited Greenfoot and Castleberg Hospital in Giggleswick on 25th September 1986 and the Chapel field, nicely clear of the hallowed cricket pitch, of course, was used for her departure by helicopter. The entire School community was formed into a giant letter V with its point at the landing site whilst many others watched from the High Rigg Road. After arrival Her Royal Highness was presented by the Deputy Lord Lieutenant of North Yorkshire to the Headmaster and Mrs Hobson and to the Head Boy, Colin Parry, and then spoke to some pupils from Paley and Style on her way to the helicopter. The Head of School called for three rousing cheers as she reached it. This was a memorable day for the Settle and Giggleswick area and it was very pleasing for Giggleswickians that the beautiful surroundings of the Chapel were shown to so large an audience.

An exchange visit between Catteral Hall and Schule Berg Hohenfels in Southern Germany created an unusual opportunity for the Chapel. The return visit took place at Whitsuntide 1987 when over 30 pupils accompanied by the Musical Director, Headmaster and his wife and two members of staff came from Germany for three days of combined music making, sightseeing and "getting to know each other". Thus on Whitsunday the Chapel was able to host a two language service in the best tradition of learning about each other's culture. The Giggleswick News Bulletin commented that this event showed the diverse use to which the Chapel could be put.

1987 also witnessed the Chapel receiving two major gifts in memory of Old Giggleswickians who had both achieved distinction and served the School over many years and in each case as

Plate 46 Some pupils coming from the Chapel framed by the Gatehouse Arch.
courtesy Giggleswick School

Plate 47 Tea on the cricket field before a service in the Chapel, OG and former parents day, 6th July 1996.

author

Chairman of the Governors for substantial terms. I have described how additional seats were provided in memory of H. M. F. Hammond and a reading desk in memory of E. H. Partridge. Further in April 1973 the Reredos had been restored and new curtains hung at the east end and at the organ loft but the 1987 gifts took the process of enhancement much further and improved the interior beauty of the building and its altar equipment most wonderfully.

Firstly the fluorescent lighting of 1947 was replaced after forty years of use. The great generosity of the gift in memory of W. H. Watson allowed the replacement of the lights to be what I, and I believe many others, wished could have been possible in 1947. Messrs Best and Lloyd of Birmingham were commissioned to carry out the renewal and through their Managing Director, Mr. John Best and their designer, Mr. Harold Shaw, working from photographs of the original chandeliers, were able to make ten new brass Flemish pendants each with seven branches for an electric light of the candle type, 1 metre high, 750mm across and weighing 24 kilograms. They are as far as practicable exact replicas of the originals and have restored the internal appearance of the building to what it originally was and also brought back the warm glow of the original gas lighting, sadly missing during the fluorescent years. I must place on record here my personal delight at seeing the new lighting on my first visit to the Chapel after its installation. I thought it was quite beautiful and the interior looked "right" once again.

Secondly new altar furniture was presented in memory of Sir Douglas Glover. This comprises a chalice and patten, an altar cross and two candlesticks and two processional candlesticks. These were designed and beautifully personally crafted by Simon Beer in sterling silver and Brazilian Rosewood and are intended to work as a family.

Dedication of these most generous gifts to the School's Chapel was afforded due ceremonial and took place at a special service on 15th November 1987 conducted by the Bishop of Bradford who spoke in his address of the way they had added to the beauty of the building.

Sadly this year so full of celebrations in and around the Chapel could not be completed without a service of the kind not too often needed in memory of an active member of staff who had died. In this case it was Stanley Simpson, a highly regarded member of the Woodwork and Metalwork Department for 15 years who had died suddenly on 11th April to the considerable shock of the School community and for whom a Memorial Service was held in the Chapel on 20th November 1987.

These events bring the story of the Chapel up to the present decade. It started as one of mixed emotions, pleasure as the Chapel approached its Centenary and anticipation over what splendid ways the events of 1897 and 1901 might in due time be celebrated counterbalanced by increasing concern about the physical condition of the building and the necessity to address the situation if, indeed, it was to be in a fit state to host any celebrations. Therefore, I have purposefully omitted from this chapter mention of two renewals of the nave roof in the fifties and in the seventies to bring the story of the major works of the nineties together in the final chapter.

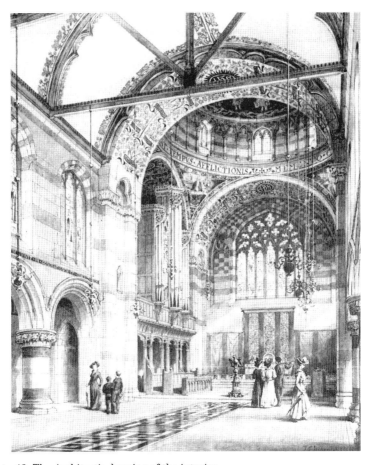

Plate 48 The Architect's drawing of the interior.

courtesy Giggleswick School

CHAPTER 6

Restoration

I have described how the Chapel was substantially constructed with
an eye to the extreme exposure of its position to the prevailing
westerly winds so often accompanied by heavy rain. After more
than fifty years the cast lead main roofs over the nave, the
transepts and the chancel had ceased to be fully weatherproof and
in 1957 were replaced. A survey made by the Lead Development
Association in 1954 reported that the lead was in good condition but
had suffered fatigue cracks arising from its movement being
restricted following temperature changes. The material chosen for
the replacement was 24 gauge traditional copper but this proved
unsatisfactory, cracks being noticed as early as 1961.

In 1970 the Copper Development Association was asked to report
and attributed the failure of the copper to metal fatigue from wind
induced vibration commenting that the width of the copper rolls
used was too wide to cope with local wind conditions (sic). Severe
star shaped cracking had occurred at the joints in the copper sheet
in particular by the rear parapet walls and around the walls
supporting the dome where wind turbulence occurs.

So a second re-roofing was carried out in 1971 using a copper
faced felt. By the late eighties there was concern that water
penetration was taking place on a significant scale evidenced by
visible interior damage, staining etc, in some places extensive. R. D.
Wolstenholme FRICS prepared condition reports on the roof as a
result of which certain pointing, flashing and rainwater discharge
system repairs and improvements were carried out seeking to
reduce the water penetration in particular into the south and west
facing masonry gable walls. His final report in October 1992,
prepared after these works had been completed, concluded that roof
replacement was again necessary and expressed serious concern

Plate 49 14th September 1996 and the scaffolding starts to grow ready for the major repairs.

author

that there might be significant deterioration of main roof beams at the west end. This was potentially a double problem – wet rot might already exist and dry rot might break out as the timbers dried out when the water ingress was stopped.

But before any action could be taken the first signs of much more worrying deterioration appeared. Small pieces of the mosaic decoration inside the dome fell off. The Governors had already commissioned Architects Vis Williams Prichard to establish the full extent of the problems with the Chapel and the measures necessary to rectify them on a thoroughly sound long term basis intended to secure it for a second century. The Architects report took time to produce as in addition to their own expertise they had deemed it appropriate to obtain expert opinions on certain aspects but by late 1994 it had become clear that the problems were extensive and the solutions would be expensive. The Governors decided to set up, amongst others, a Chapel Appeal Working Party which had its inaugural meeting on 14th January 1995. Firstly it agreed unanimously that retention, and thus full restoration, of the Chapel was the first priority for any funds which might be raised. They considered it was the School's principal and most admired building and that it played a central part in the ethos of the School community. Also discussed at this meeting was the uncertain extent of the damage to the backing of the mosaic in the dome and, to protect choir and officiating clergy from any catastrophic collapse, scaffolding was quickly erected giving both a roof over the area under the dome and a platform from which the cause and extent of the problem could be determined, and ultimately remedied. With safety properly paramount the necessity for this cannot be questioned in any way but it was sad to see the interior disfigured by rough metal and wood, the wonderful mosaics in the dome obscured and natural light in the building severely reduced. As time progressed the level of this roof/floor was raised and its extent was reduced to the base and actual diameter of the dome respectively.

The Architect's findings suggested expenditure of £500,000 would be necessary to carry out full restoration of the building and site, although this could be split into segments of varying importance. Making the building watertight and bringing to an end the constant saturation of certain parts of the masonry was the first vital priority. As the watertightness of the dome was no longer certain Rowan Technologies Ltd were retained and Dr. D. M. Farrell took ultrasonic readings to establish the degree of thinning of its copper covering. He found the detail of the dome to be excellent with drainage channels built into the welts between the sheets of copper but in places there was a major thinning of the sheeting such that replacement was unavoidable. The felt cover over the other roof areas was also judged to be life expired and the whole of the roof drainage system, flashing, gutters, hoppers and fall pipes was found to be defective and causing water to flow over surfaces it should not. Extensive pointing of walls and window surrounds to prevent water access by these avenues was also a necessity, as well as re-setting of coping stones. Most householders will be aware that water penetration can take place when strong wind and rain combine which does not occur at other times and that the external point of ingress of the rain water is often distant from its materialisation inside and very difficult to find. The Chapel suffers many more days of wind driven rain than the average house and it arrives undeflected from the Irish Sea. It was also established that the boiler flue gasses in the revised flue arrangements installed together with a new gas fired boiler in 1982 were seriously contributing to condensation damage to the west end gable wall.

Only with these "vital" works approved and completed would there be any purpose in addressing the consequences of the dampness inside the building. The major problem was the mosaic in the dome where the backing render had failed in several places consistent with water penetration and dampness therefrom rising behind the mosaic. Here also the Architects sought expert opinion, this time from Dr. Norman Tennant, a visiting researcher from Strathclyde University, formerly Scientific Conservation Officer at the Burrell Collection, Glasgow and the acknowledged expert in this field, who had been advising English Heritage and also the Westminster Cathedral Authorities about mosaic work carried out at the same time as that at Giggleswick. In readiness to implement Dr Tennant's recommendations specialist firms were identified to carry out refixing of the loose parts or, as the very last resort, complete replacement. Dr. Tennant had indicated his interest in giving advice on this problem but could not do so until his return from a lecture tour in the USA and thus his opinions were not available during early 1995. The size (114 square metres) and quality of the mosaic work had clearly surprised the Architects when they saw it for, in the presentation to the European Commission, they wrote that mosaic work is rare in the UK and that it was even more surprising to find a mosaic of this scale and quality tucked away at this corner at the edge of the Yorkshire Dales National Park more usually associated with untameable moorland, sheep, rural industry and tourism. It is therefore an important work and merits the expenditure required to restore it. In March 1996 a revised breakdown of estimated costs included £103,000 for mosaic repairs. (See Appendix 8)

71

Plate 50 The temporary cover under which the roof renewal was carried out and which was such a conspicuous feature in the landscape from October 1996 to January 1997. Pictured on 28th November 1996

author

Plate 51 Another view of the tent.

author

Water ingress damage had also affected parts of the sgraffito work which could be re-worked to the original patterns and to stonework which would need to be cleaned. General redecoration, internal repointing round metal windows, rewiring, a new fire detection system and re-plastering with a waterproof additive up to 1 metre height in the vestry to counteract a limited rising damp problem completed the interior proposals. It was also suggested a toilet be created in the vestry area using modern electrical equipment which would not need a septic tank.

Works proposed for the site included a certain amount of upgrading by providing a tarmac surface to the access road and car park and a gravel surface to the path to the vestry, stone edged and using edging stones to create suitable steps. A new water supply was also proposed. The electricity supply was first provided in 1947 and its renewal was proposed.

The building was given Grade II* listed status in 1958 and therefore certain grants were potentially available, especially European Commission funds during 1995 for restoration of religious monuments. The Architects prepared a submission to obtain some of these funds which, with support in Brussels from the Euro MP for the School's constituency, Mr. Edward McMillan-Scott, duly acknowledged in the Chapel Centenary Appeal brochure, gained a grant of £50,000 ECU or about £40,000. This triggered a further Grant of £68,000 from English Heritage. Such Grants are basically awarded to offset the cost of repairing listed buildings with the same materials as originally used, or in certain cases modern materials made to look the same as the originals, when modern materials used in a modern way would be substantially cheaper and there is no benefit to the owner from not so doing. Therefore for the Grants to be confirmed the new main roofs would once again be of lead and the dome would be recovered in copper. In addition to the Grants certain Old Giggleswickians who knew of the problems donated £44,000 before the need was generally made known.

The Governors decided that the Appeal to raise the rest of the money needed would be addressed to Old Giggleswickians. It was appropriate, therefore, to launch it on Old Giggleswickians Day 1996, Saturday 6th July and some special events were arranged for the occasion hosted by the Chairman of the Governors, Lord Shuttleworth. After the President of the OG Club's Reception in the Dutton Centre a quite magnificent buffet lunch was provided by the School caterers in a large yellow and white flower-bedecked marquee put up in the sports hall – better known to the older OGs as the covered playground. Lord Shuttleworth and the Headmaster addressed the gathering formally to launch the appeal stressing that, extraordinary and beautiful though the building is it is an essential part of School life as the place of worship. After the luncheon the Chapel was open for visitors to inspect a comprehensive exhibition covering its construction, its history and much memorabilia, largely from the Brayshaw collection and featuring some large sized prints of photographs taken during the construction period as well as some of the Architects own drawings. It was particularly interesting whilst inside the building to study the photographs taken during construction and so understand how the familiar completed structure was formed.

By this time the scaffold platform had been raised to its final level with access by ladders having an intermediate platform. The first ladder rose from the south gallery pews to the platform which was cantilevered out towards the centre of the building, the second ladder rising from its outer end and passing through a hole in the scaffold platform some fifty feet above the marble floor. Visitors with strong nerves were invited, for a large donation to the Chapel Appeal (and an even larger one to come down again), to climb these ladders, supported by the Clerk to the Governors and Bursar, Denis Smith, an experienced climber, assisted by members of the School climbing club, to inspect the damage to the mosaic at close quarters. I found it a fascinating experience, providing some new perspectives of the Chapel and, although I was disappointed to find the mosaic covered over, the large areas which were loose or missing could easily be seen whilst so close a view of the lantern was a rare treat. But on stepping out over the hole onto the ladder to come back down the belaying rope was more than a little comforting. The Chapel had found another role – a very imposing exhibition hall.

By August the fund had reached £231,000 and the Governors were in a position to give the go-ahead for the vital first phase works, recladding of the dome, recovering of the main roofs, overhauling the roof drainage system and the essential pointing. Work began quickly.

The Chapel found yet another role in a money raising event to fund its repairs when from Friday 13th to Sunday 15th September 1996 there was a Festival of Flowers and Music. The flower part of this festival was the placing all round the building of twenty flower arrangements by members of the North Craven Flower Club, two of which were sponsored by local Settle firms. Their titles and arrangers were set out in a programme, the detail presented as Appendix 9.

A separate programme detailed the Music part of the festival which started on Friday evening with a concert "Words and Music for September" whose ticket price included a Reception with wine and canapés in the Dutton Centre. On Saturday there was a different type of music on the hour each hour from 9.00am to 4.00pm except 1.00pm. At that hour a ploughman's lunch was available in a marquee on the cricket field with Dixieland jazz accompaniment by the Black Horse Jazzmen. At 7.30pm the highlight of the festival was a piano recital by Kathryn Stott of music by Grieg, Chopin, Ravel and Rachmaninov, tickets for this including a fork supper in the Dutton Centre at which the Recitalist was present. On Sunday there were various styles of music again, at 10.30am, 11.00am and then hourly until 3.00pm culminating with a performance at 5.00pm of Faure's "Requiem" by present and former members of Giggleswick's Choir and Orchestra. It was a weekend of beautiful Autumn weather and on Saturday when I made my visit it was delightful indeed to sit in the sun enjoying my lunch listening to the Jazzmen in those beautiful surroundings.

By the weekend of these events there was visible evidence that restoration was under way with scaffolding growing round the Chapel. Eventually this enclosed the whole roof area and the higher parts of the walls being covered with white polythene sheeting clearing the maximum height of the lantern over the dome and thus more than 100 feet above the ground. As the Chapel stands on high ground this large white "tent" was far more dominant in the landscape than the green dome had ever been, and, I'm sure not untypically, as I arrived at Settle on the train one day some passengers had noticed and were commenting on it.

During one of my research visits to the School I gathered during conversation that the work had taken somewhat longer than planned and disappointment was being felt that the scaffolding would not be taken down in time for the Carol Service in mid December. My "eyes" in Settle phoned me on 10th January 1997 to say that the tent had gone and a brown dome was now visible. This reappearance of the Architects original vision of his building merited an urgent trip to admire it and obtain a photographic record. The forecast for 14th January was very good suggesting sunshine giving unseasonably high temperatures and I spent a very pleasant hour taking pictures from almost every angle. There was still scaffolding at most of the main walls and the repointing work was still on-going. The total expenditure thus far had been roundly £300,000.

The Craven Herald and Pioneer reported on Friday 31st January 1997 under the heading "School spends a few bob on copper" that Giggleswick's famous landmark had changed colour and that the flash of pastel green so long used by walkers and motorist (and flyers) to check their locations had gone being replaced by a copper

Plate 52 Damage to the mosaic inside the dome.

courtesy Giggleswick School

Plate 53 A closer view of some of the damage.

courtesy Giggleswick School

76

Plate 54 A close up of part of the damage to the mosaic.

courtesy Giggleswick School

Plate 55 A close up of damage to the rainwater goods.

courtesy Giggleswick School

colour. They thus probably printed the first colour photograph of the Chapel in the form its architect conceived, unusually a view taken from the Northwest.

The temporary roof had been recommended by the Architects to enable the timbers under the roof covering to be exposed for a possibly prolonged period for examination. The estimates allowed for 15% replacement of the boarding under the main roofs but until these were uncovered the time required for any drying out and any treatment or replacement found necessary could not be known. The possibility that treatment of the main beams might be necessary was also a factor in the recommendation. Kirk Scaffolds of Padiham were the scaffolding contractors responsible for that remarkable change to the local landscape.

With the dome uncovered the routes of water penetration and the extent of problems there could be identified so that, once the re-roofing was complete, restoration of the mosaic could be considered. By this time the measures needed had been clarified and, happily, the estimated expenditure had reduced, now being £40,000. Adequate funds for this were available allowing the work to be authorised early in 1997 with completion achieved by early Summer. The other internal restorations and renovations had to await drying out of the masonry and plaster work but it was intended they would be complete in time for the events planned to celebrate the centenary of the laying of the Foundation stone on 7th October 1897.

It is one of those odd coincidences that the Old Giggleswickians Club was founded in the year the Chapel was started so that the Annual Club Dinner held at the School, currently in March, was in 1997 a special "centenary" one. A sad event was associated with the dinner. L. P. Dutton, the second of those three long serving Second Masters had died on 13th January and a memorial service for him was held in the Chapel on the afternoon of Saturday 22nd March. I was not present but heard that it was a very moving event. The special guest at the dinner was the retiring Chairman of Governors, Lord Shuttleworth, whose 13 year tenure had (amongst much else) seen the Chapel's problems emerge, the estimates of repair costs presented, the decision taken that the building remained essential to the School's requirements and the successful appeal launched. Thus his leadership ensured that, in its centenary year, the fabric was once again in first class condition and making good the damage to the artistically important internal decoration could be undertaken. Opportunity was also taken at the dinner to make the first formal announcement that the celebration of the Foundation Stone Centenary would be on Sunday 5th October 1997. Present and former pupils will feature in a full programme of events in the Chapel. For this very special day OGs notable in their professions are available to fill the necessary roles and thus the Preacher at the special Chapel Centenary service will be The Rev'd Dr John Platt, Chaplain of Pembroke College, Oxford. In the afternoon a recital of songs composed contemporaneously with the Chapel's construction will be given by Sarah Fox, 1997 winner of the prestigious Kathleen Ferrier Award, after which the Sports Hall will again sport a marquee for a Special Centenary Buffet. In the evening Richard Whiteley will present a Centenary Celebration in words and music of the Life and Times of Giggleswick Chapel. There is a suggestion the final part of this may be in candlelight as a reminder of those Last Night of Term services.

These events, yet to be savoured, bring the Chapel's first hundred years to a close. Great expenditure has been needed to secure its continuance as the spiritual centre of the School and great generosity has been shown, especially by the School's former pupils, to provide the funds needed. The result is that a beautiful and remarkable building will, when the interior renovation is complete, once again be as its designer intended, something for the School to be proud of and something to be admired by all with an interest in architecture and art.

Compared with the past it plays an increasing role in the life of the local community with joint religious services as well as musical and dramatic events. For example May 1997 will see a confirmation service for both School pupils and local children . Such events ensure the beauty of the building is brought to the notice of a much larger population than was hitherto customary.

But its primary function, that for which Walter Morrison gave it to the School and which justified the School authorities decision to find the money for the major repairs, is as the School's place of worship and the centre of its spiritual life. Increasingly I am becoming aware that my feeling for the building is less unusual than I imagined and one aim of this book is to prompt happy memories for those who have experienced the building as a regular place of worship as well as chronicle its origins and describe its artistic features.

It is my hope that Giggleswick School Chapel will continue for another century to be the core of the affection Old Giggleswickians have for the School and the superb countryside in which it stands and that, like myself, future School boys and now, girls, may be enchanted by its site, exceptional interior and traditions.

Plate 56 The marquee on the cricket field during the Festival of Flowers and Music weekend, 14th September 1996.

author

Plate 57 14th January 1997 and the new copper dome gleams in unseasonal sunshine.

author

Dimensions of the Building

	Ft.	ins.
Exterior east to west, including buttresses (taken above the plinth)	108	6
Exterior north to south, across transepts (including buttresses above the plinth)	62	0
Interior east to west, excluding antechapel	83	0
Interior north to south across transepts	48	0
Interior north to south through nave and aisle	42	0
Span of roof and drum	28	0
Height from floor to wall plate of nave	28	6
Height from floor to crown of nave ceiling	40	0
Height from floor to cornice below drum	41	7
Height from floor to springing of dome	52	5
Height from floor to crown of dome at eye of lantern	68	9
Exterior height from floor of vestry to top of cross on lantern	93	0

Plate 58 Construction in progress during 1897- 8 : the West Wall from the North East.

courtesy Giggleswick School (Brocklebank Collection)

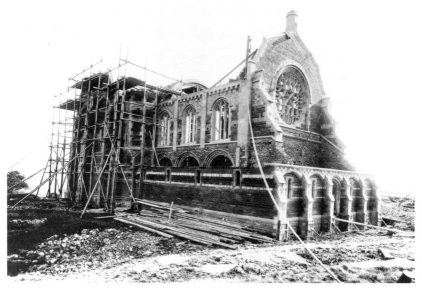

Plate 59 A view from the South East of the work in progress.

courtesy Giggleswick School (Brocklebank Collection)

Analysis of Building Accounts April 1902

CONSTRUCTION				£	s	d
Payments for day labour and materials on the building and approaches				14,614	4	6
WORK UNDER CONTRACTS						
Iron and Brass work				261	16	9
Wood Flooring				19	16	1
Dome , Masonry				587	10	0
Plumbing				962	0	0
Concrete Floor				251	15	0
Carpentry				1,017	19	6
Joinery				486	10	0
Safe Door				23	0	0
Heating and Ventilation				149	15	0
Lightning Conductor				44	10	0
TOTAL COST OF CONSTRUCTION				18,418	16	10
DECORATION	£	s	d			
Wood Carving	635	12	0			
Stone Carving	402	12	0			
Marble Floor	286	9	4			
	1,324	13	4	1,324	13	4
Mosaics				3,633	1	7
Statues				450	0	0
Stained Glass				1,426	3	5
Sgraffito Work				183	13	5
				7,017	11	7
FURNITURE						
Furniture including cupboards, tables, chairs, hassocks etc				317	16	9
Gas fittings				554	18	3
Organ and case				1,380	6	0
				2,253	1	0
TOTAL COST OF CHAPEL				27,689	9	7
OTHER BUILDINGS						
CRICKET PAVILION						
Cost of building				1,351	2	1
Clock and terraces				262	11	8
TOTAL				1,613	13	9
GATEHOUSE						
Cost of building				1,342	2	6
Approaches, walls and yard				171	15	2
TOTAL				1,513	17	8
TOTAL COST OF WORKS				30,817	1	0

Specification of Organ

GREAT ORGAN

1	Open Diapason	8 ft
2	Wald Flute	8 ft
3	Dulciana	8 ft
4	Principal	4 ft
5	Stopped Flute	4 ft
6	Twelfth	$2^2/_3$ ft
7	Fifteenth	2 ft
8	Mixture	3 ranks (19-22-26)

SWELL

9	Violin Diapason	8 ft
10	Lieblich Flute	8 ft
11	Gamba	8 ft
12	Gemshorn	4 ft
13	Flageolet	2 ft
14	Mixture	2 ranks (12-15)
15	Contra Oboe	16 ft
16	Trumpet	8 ft

CHOIR

17	Gedacht	8 ft
18	Nason	4 ft
19	Nazard	$2^2/_3$ ft
20	Piccolo	2 ft
21	Tierce	$1^3/_5$ ft
22	Clarinet	8 ft

PEDAL

23	Sub Bass	32 ft
24	Violone	16 ft
25	Bourdon	16 ft
26	Principal	8 ft
27	Bass Flute	8 ft
28	Fifteenth	4 ft
29	Octave Flute	4 ft
30	Piccolo	2 ft

COUPLERS

Swell to Great	—	mechanical
Swell to Choir	—	mechanical
Great to Pedal	—	mechanical
Swell to Pedal	—	mechanical
Choir to Pedal	—	mechanical
Great to Pedal Piston	—	pneumatic

APPENDIX 4

Inauguration of the Organ

GIGGLESWICK SCHOOL

Friday 4th October at 4pm
in the new Chapel given by Mr. Morrison to the School

ORGAN RECITAL
by
Sir Walter Parratt, Mus. Doc.
Master of the King's Music

PROGRAMME

1	Overture Tolomeo	Handel
2	Largo from the New World Symphony	Dvorák
3	Prelude and Fugue in D Major	J. S. Bach
4	Canon in B Minor	Schumann
5	Fantasie in E Flat	Saint Saëns
6	Andante in A Flat	John Stainer
7	Schiller March	Meyerbeer

The recital ended there will be an opportunity of looking round
the Chapel; and afterwards there will be tea in Big School.

Memorials inside the Chapel

North side of altar
>Memorial tablet to Rev. George Style MA
>Headmaster 1869-1904

South side of altar
also four wooden panels behind choir stalls on North side
>"In memoriam" 1939-45 War

North side aisle, east to west – Tablets
>1. Sydney Arthur Slater, Lt. Imperial Yeomanry
>   Died South Africa 1901
>2. John Druville Slater, Died 23rd March 1915, Aged 12
>3. James Micah Birtwhistle, Died 16th June 1910, Aged 14

South side aisle, west to east – Tablets
>1. Gifford Bromley Mannock Assistant Master
>   1874 until his death 26th May 1908
>2. Stephani Pellatt Smith died MDCCCCV

Main Pillar facing the Pulpit
>"In memoriam" 1914-19 War

Additional seating in aisles
>H.M.F. Hammond 1896 – 1945
>also a brass tablet affixed to the Second Masters stall.

APPENDIX 6

"Punch" commented on the 1927 Solar Eclipse with the following verse, choosing to mention Giggleswick no doubt because the Astronomer Royal made his observations there.

LAUS LUNAE

["As the moon's shadow peeped over the sun's face
cheers were raised". *Morning Papers, 29th June*].

MYRIADS of bards, O MOON, have sung thy grace,
Sweet regent of the sky, unquestioned queen
Among the lesser lights, in silver sheen
Climbing the skies with sad and silent pace;
And some have dared thy glories to abase
By likening them to cheese grown old and green,
Or feign to see upon thy orb serene
The features of a comic human face.
But of all tributes paid thee by the lips
Of seer or savage, in ten thousand years,
The strangest and most nobly lunatic
Was when, at that first moment of eclipse,
Thy onset woke enthusiastic cheers
From the rapt revellers at Giggleswick.

Punch, or the London Charivari
6th July 1927

APPENDIX 7

Recital on the Chapel Organ
by
Dr. Francis Jackson
Organist York Minster
Saturday 15th July 1961

Following reconditioning work on which
he had given technical advice

PROGRAMME

1	Fantasia in F Minor K608	Mozart
2	Toccata and Fugue in D Major	J. S. Bach
3	Sonata (No. 3) for Organ	Hindemith
4	Diversion for mixtures	Jackson
5	Toccata (1953)	Gordon Phillips
6	Voluntary in E	Samuel Wesley
7	Variations sur un Noel (Op. 20)	Marcel Dupré

Plate 60 Another view of the new copper dome on 14th January 1997.

author

Plate 61 The Chapel from the North East, much the same aspect as the Architecht's drawing presented as the frontispiece. Photographed on 14th January 1997.

author

Summary of Chapel Refurbishment Costs March 1996

PHASE 1 COSTS		£
Dome and Cupola – Copper		35,000
Scaffolding/weather protection		15,000
Mansard Roofs – Code 5 Lead		70,000
Associated roofing works –	repointing, gutters rain water pipes, flashings scaffolding of lower roofs	43,000
External walls – repointing etc		18,000
Stabilisation of Mosaic		6,000
Contingency		20,000
		207,000

PHASE 2 COSTS		
Internal Works –	replastering, new toilet, decoration, sgraffito repairs, new electric supply, stone cleaning, fire detection system, repair to vestry etc.	48,000
Mosaic		103,000
External Works –	including access roads, footpaths, car park, buttresses, windows, boiler	69,000
		220,000
Plus professional fees and VAT thereon		76,516
	Gross Total	503,516

It was hoped the VAT would be recoverable

APPENDIX 9

Festival of Flowers in the Chapel
13th 14th 15th September 1996

Title	Arrangers
1 September Garlands	Pauline Burgon, Sue Taylor Shirley Thornton
2 English Country Gardens	Joan Brown, Sheila Glossop Mary Metcalf, Mary Thwaite
3 Jesus Christ Superstar	Margaret Sangster
4 The Holly and the Ivy	Christine Brown, Jennifer Hill
5 Moonlight Serenade	Enid Caton
6 Romeo and Juliet/ Midsummer Night's Dream	Becky Sanderson
7 Nights in the Gardens of Spain Arrangement sponsored by Dukes of Settle	Margaret Hamby, Mary Loydall
8 The Four Seasons	Susan Fairhurst
9 Serenade for Strings	Joan Barker
10 Rhythm and Blues	Judy Harpham
11 Fanfare Arrangement sponsored by Dugdales of Settle	Barbara Johnson
12 Royal Fireworks Music	Pam Jordan
13 The Magic Flute	Pam Hall, Emily Moran
14 Viennese Waltz	Fiona Newhouse
15 Madam Butterfly	Diane Kellow, Joan Mason
16 Gilbert and Sullivan	Margaret Sunderland
17 Swan Lake/ Handel's Water Music	Dorothy Ashworth, Pat Hainsworth Jenny Preston
18 Requiem	Joan Burke
19 Night and Day	Wyn Wiseman
20 Phantom of the Opera	Alice Whaites

Arrangement No. 1 was placed at the north side of the antechapel No. 2 inside the main nave doors Nos. 3 to 10 along the north side of the building, No. 6 in the Pulpit and No.8 below the dome. Nos. 11 and 12 were north and south of the altar whilst Nos. 13 to 20 were along the south side of the building, No. 20 being at the west end of the south aisle.

Plate 62 The light outside the Chapel's West door decorated for the Festival of Flowers and Music, 14th September 1996.

author

Schedule of Proposed External Repairs 1995

The numbers were used to illustrate the site of each type of work on a series of plans of each elevation. The North and South elevations follow as plan B.

1 The replacement of the original 24 gauge copper roof covering of the dome and lantern.

2 The replacement of the copper gauze faced felt roof covering to the mansard aisle, Chapel and transept roofs.

3 The repair of structural timber where necessary in the various inaccessible and concealed areas of the roof.

4 Roof repairs which involve the carrying up of the proposed roof finish behind the hidden gable parapet walls. The present gable parapets are exposed on two faces and therefore by extending the new roof coverings on the hidden back face the degree of exposure of those walls will be reduced.

5 The coping stones to these gables require to be re-set and repointed. Where possible the introduction of the DPC or capping will be introduced under the coping.

6 Renewal of all cappings and masonry pointing around the lantern clerestory of the dome, abutments and stone towers.

7 The renewal of rain water goods where hopper heads and pipework have suffered from bi-metallic corrosion or have rusted through.

8 The principal areas of damp affected wall are those which face the south or west into the prevailing wind or where rainwater goods or flues are not functioning correctly.

9 All other masonry cap flashings will require to be checked and replaced in lead where necessary.

10 The completion of the repointing programme to the stonework particularly to the more difficult tightly jointed ashlar blocks which appear not to have been repointed since the building was first built.

11 The principal boiler flue which has been in continuous use for 96 years requires complete reinstatement. The flue is on the south elevation gable wall and is responsible for causing visible dampness internally to large areas of the wall due to the recurring condensation when the boilers are fired.

12 Repointing to the window surrounds is necessary.

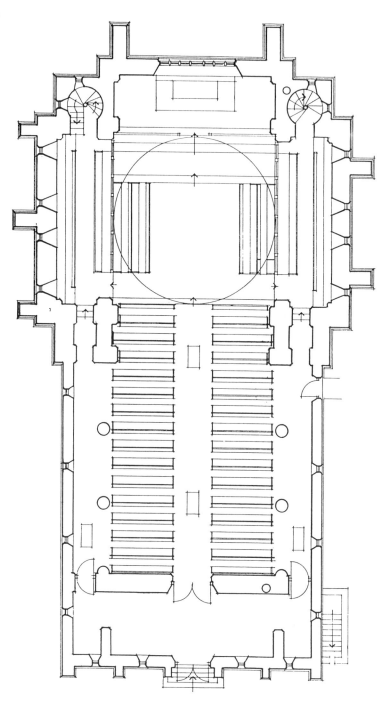

GROUND FLOOR

PLAN B

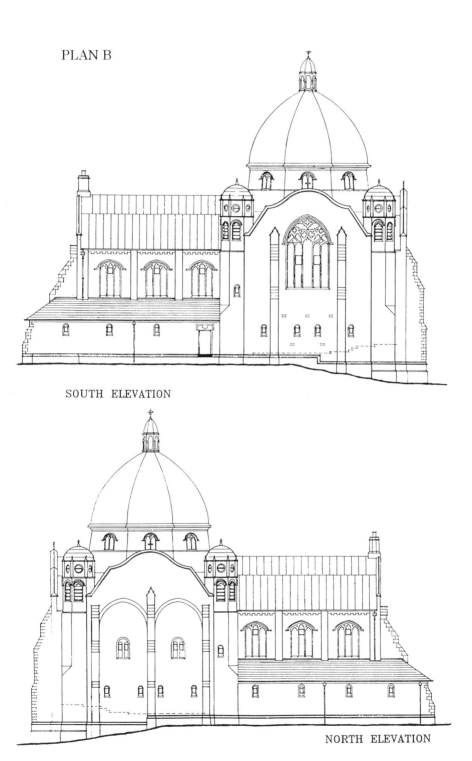

SOUTH ELEVATION

NORTH ELEVATION

95

Plate 63 The cricket field and Chapel, with the Southern Ribblesdale hills beyond, from the North West.

courtesy Giggleswick School